*g*arden**M**ania

philip de bay & james bolton

garden Mania

the ardent gardener's compendium of design & decoration

with a preface by monty don

CLARKSON POTTER / PUBLISHERS
New York

On the cover A Dutch formal garden, *c.* 1700.

Half title A French fashion plate of 1799 by Vernet: a lady of the Directoire sporting a revolutionary floral bonnet.

Frontispiece A view from the terrace of the nineteenth-century Italianate gardens at Shrubland, Suffolk, England.

This page A French Baroque design by Jean Le Pautre for a nymph supporting a flowering urn.

Copyright © 2000 by The Stapleton Collection
Design and picture selection copyright © 2000 by
Thames & Hudson Ltd., London

Published by Clarkson Potter/Publishers,
New York, New York.
Member of the Crown Publishing Group.

Random House Inc. New York, Toronto, London, Sydney,
Auckland

www.randomhouse.com

CLARKSON N. POTTER is a trademark and POTTER and
colophon are registered trademarks of Random House, Inc.

Originally published in Great Britain by
Thames & Hudson Ltd., London, in 2000.

Library of Congress Cataloging-in-Publication Data
available upon request from the publisher.

ISBN 0-609-80728-5

10 9 8 7 6 5 4 3 2 1

First American Edition

Printed and bound in China

Contents

Preface by Monty Don

Gardening in the twenty-first century is by and large an urban activity and has therefore become most people's closest contact with 'nature'. Enormous store is set by the amount of wildlife that can be induced to share our small back-gardens. Yet it is a measure of how far modern man lives from the influence of the natural world that he looks for it in his garden. After all, from the first, every garden has been a manifestation of man's need to control and tame nature. The garden of Eden was fashioned from the first in man's image. The fall from grace was a measure of bad gardening as much as eye-popping sexual awareness. Can fallen man make a perfect garden? Certainly, as this book shows, we have been trying for a very long time.

Looking through the collection of illustrations that Philip de Bay has gathered for this book, I am struck by how ill at ease most of the humans are, parading around their highly ornate and structured defiance of the forces of nature around them. In the portraits of formal gardens human activity is restricted to a slow perambulation. Any evidence of the frenzied activity of the teams of gardeners needed to maintain that static image is unusual, although they do exist. My favourite is on pages 372–73, where workers at the Prince of Lichtenstein's garden near Vienna are bringing out orange trees. The overturned empty barrel and dumped roller and rake fire the formal array of topiary and tender greens with an utterly modern and familiar gardening reality. The main exceptions to this rule, as on pages 286–87, are pictures of human activity with the gardens merely a backdrop, created like a stage set for a masque. This, I think, is the clue to the enduring power of gardening: at its core it is an entirely human activity. After all, nature hardly needs us to grow its own. All the devices and conceits that this book so wonderfully illustrates are part of the instinctive human desire to tame and reclaim their domestic space away from nature rather than to share it with the natural world.

And yet what makes gardening in all its forms so richly satisfying is the way that, out of the constant conflict of man's desire to control and order his world and the inherent uncontrollability of the natural world around him, comes a genuine creative expression. Making a garden has always been one of the grandest and yet most available of all art forms. This book is a chronicle of the desire not to repress nature but to make something of it in man's own image, and there is something heroic about the vanity and folly of this. As a result, as one who is self-confessedly mad about gardening, I find *Garden Mania* a wonderfully sane celebration of the essential vein of humanity that runs right through the heart of every garden.

Page 6 An eighteenth-century fashion plate from the *Galérie des Modes*, showing trellis and topiary.

7

Introduction Garden Mania

Gardens have been a source of delight, desire and pleasure for centuries. The urge to control and to enjoy nature, to create an earthly
paradise, through the designs, the ornaments, the flowers and the
shrubs which combine to make up the garden is one of the most
delightful of human manias. Over the centuries this obsession with
horticultural delight has taken many forms and expressions, from
the architectural delights of the Baroque gardens of Italy, via the
vistas and parterres of Versailles, to the herbaceous borders of
village England. It has also been recorded in the prints and albums
of large-scale and small-scale garden designs from which the hun-
dreds of fascinating images reproduced in this book are drawn, to
create a feast for the practising and the armchair gardener.

Here are the fruits of expert plantsmanship: parterres, hedges,
mazes and topiary. Here, too, are the architectural forms of weird
and wonderful structures in wood, stone and metal. Temples,
pavilions, conservatories, orangeries, follies, mausoleums and
ruins are countered on the human scale by statuary, urns and every
style of wooden structure – Gothick, Classical, Moorish and Oriental. Ingenious swings and helter-skelters, pigeon-houses, aviaries
and menageries extend the delights of this place of amusement and
surprise – the garden.

Gardens have always been made for enjoyment, whether aesthetic or as the providers of comestibles. They are distractions
from the realities of everyday life and the outside world. From the
earliest Persian garden, turned resolutely in on itself, to the modest

present-day suburban garden, their purpose is to soothe, refresh and invigorate. In Ancient Egypt, the Pharaoh was rowed across garden pools by girls clad only in gold nets. In Sicily, Archimedes created a floating garden with shady walks and ornamental water. The Emperor Hadrian constructed a sumptuous dining-room at his villa at Tivoli, where his guests reclined and feasted amid cascades and other water features. In medieval England, gardens were for lovers, who reclined on turf benches and bathed together in pools under elaborate fountains.

The garden is a place of display, nurtured carefully by the obsessive gardener: the colours of flowers, the sparkling of water in fountains and cascades, the gleam of white marble. The ear is delighted by the trickle of a rill or the calling and singing of birds in the trees or nearby aviary. And to intensify the gratification of the senses, what better than to array this paradise regained with ingenious ornaments to amuse and beguile the visitor and guest?

Display and delight were undoubtedly uppermost in the minds of the designers and architects of the sixteenth- and seventeenth-century gardens of Italy, lavishly ornamental in deliberate imitation of the glories of Ancient Rome. The gardens at the Villa d'Este, for instance, designed in the 1560s, harnessed the waters of the river Aniene to provide a profusion of fountains and pools, water staircases and cascades. Statues were taken from the ruins of Hadrian's Villa nearby to adorn the garden and to give additional significance to the lavish display. Images of Hercules, the mythical ancestor of the d'Este family, featured prominently. In places, visitors were offered a moral choice: the path of virtue, represented by the grotto of Diana, or the path of vice in the form of the grotto of Venus. Ingenious hydraulic devices caused mechanical birds to sing or organs to play, or set off jets to soak the unwary guest.

Above Detail of bird from an early eighteenth-century print.

As fashion-conscious Europe turned to French styles of architecture and decoration in the mid seventeenth century, so France became the centre of garden mania in the grand style during the same period. At Vaux-le-Vicomte in 1653, Louis XIV's minister, Nicolas Fouquet, employed Le Nôtre to create a colossal garden of regal magnificence. Fouquet invited the king to a spectacular fête in the garden, which Louis described as 'insolent and audacious'. Fouquet's fate was sealed; he was imprisoned, and the plants and ornaments of his sumptuous gardens were transferred to Versailles. Louis also retained the services of Le Nôtre. At Versailles, ornament was deeply political, symbolizing the glory of the Sun King and reflecting the power and prestige of France.

Versailles mania spread across Europe. No prince or princeling worthy of his title was content until he too had remodelled his garden in imitation of Le Nôtre. In Vienna, the Hapsburgs rebuilt Schönbrunn, which like Versailles had originally been a hunting-lodge, deliberately to rival the French original. Parterres stretch into the distance and high walls of clipped trees divide the garden into squares and rectangles. In Germany, Schwetzingen boasted a vast circular parterre with curved trellis arches.

Garden mania is bipartite; it thrives on the interplay and alternation of the formal and informal. The fountains and parterres, steps and terraces, bosquets and arbours all so fashionable in the late seventeenth century and in the early eighteenth were bound to provoke a reaction. With political power shifting northwards after the death of Louis XIV, so the revolt against formality and classicism first began in England.

Decoration returned in the early years of the nineteenth century; terraces with balustrades of stone or wrought-iron and even fountains reappeared. Of the many varied styles which proliferated, none was as popular as the 'Italianate'. Shrubland Park, where the garden was laid out by the eminent Victorian

Above Detail of horned beetle from an early eighteenth-century print.

architect Sir Charles Barry, was dominated by an enormous stair-case of 137 steps which carried the visitor down the escarpment to the lower terrace. In the United States, Edith Wharton's books on Italian villas created a craze for this style among the newly rich, determined to display their wealth. The Villa Vizcaya in Florida, partly based on the Villa Lante, is a remarkable reproduction of a sixteenth-century Italian garden; among the parterres and *allées* of evergreen oak, a stone boat floats in the sea just off-shore from a formal terrace. Dumbarton Oaks in Washington D.C., by the designer Beatrix Farrand, looks like an Italian design out of the Arts and Crafts Movement!

Technological advances during the nineteenth century gave the ardent horticulturalist a much wider range of materials with which to ornament a garden. A Mrs. Coade of Lambeth invented a ceramic-based artificial stone (whose composition has defied analysis until recently). Cast-iron enjoyed its moment of fashion as the new material in an age which delighted in experimentation.

Long, golden Edwardian afternoons seemed to have character-ized the opening decade of the twentieth century, at least in retrospect. The architect Edwin Lutyens designed fabulously detailed and costly houses and gardens for his patrons in styles ranging from what might be termed Surrey Vernacular to the severely Classical.

For the remainder of the century, garden mania developed a leaning towards the instant. Immediate effects responded to the desire for violent visual assault. Walls are painted vibrant blue or purple. Pools, cascades, trees and shrubs are illuminated to dra-matize the garden after dark. Even television sets are incorporated into the designs. New plants are bred by plant breeders to gratify the desire for novelty; new devices and gadgets are invented to care for them. And every new feature is obsessively pursued by garden-ers driven by age-old habits and desires.

1
Shaping
Nature

A Paradise on Earth

All growing and living elements of the garden can be trained, clipped, sheared, pleached, espaliered, cordoned and pruned, or left to grow into an imitation of the wild. Soil can be moved to create patterns and forms, such as amphitheatres or even garden theatres. The more formal the garden the greater the importance and popularity of planting and the shaping of nature in the form of parterres, hedges, topiary, mazes and even living trellis.

The creation of ground-level designs, using evergreen plants, was introduced by the Romans. The Renaissance and Baroque gardens of Italy used box, rosemary and bay in square patterns, embellished with lemon trees in terracotta pots. The parterre reached its finest expression in seventeenth- and eighteenth-century France: miles of dwarf box were formed into geometric and paisley shapes, set against a permanent background of coloured stones and gravel. The French also perfected the clipping of hedges. The gardens of Versailles contained eight million hornbeams trained into seemingly endless hedge around the woodland planting on each side of the main *allées*. The hedges were some-

Opposite Detail of a *parterre de broderie* design from
Johann Van Der Groen's *The Netherlandish Gardener* (1699).

13

times given a spectacularly architectural appearance as colon-nades, palissades, arches, columns and whole *cabinets de verdures*.

Opus topiarium was the Roman art of ornamental gardening, of which the clipping of trees and shrubs was only a part. In Roman gardens, hunting scenes or fleets of ships might be cut from cypresses, or even the garden owner's name formed from box. The fashion of clipping evergreens reappeared in the Middle Ages; shrubs might be trimmed into layers like gigantic wedding cakes. The fifteenth-century gardens of the Villa Rucellai in Italy were full of spheres, porticoes, temples, vases, urns, apes, donkeys, oxen, a bear, giants (of both sexes), all formed from various evergreens.

From the seventeenth century, pattern-books were published in the major European countries showing how the adventurous shears-wielding gardener could go about designing and creating his own paradise. All sorts of plants were advocated for the creation of splendid havens of peace. According to one English writer, rosemary was especially popular among women topiarists. The clipping fashion declined in the eighteenth century, to be revived by the Arts and Crafts Movement in the late nineteenth century.

Perhaps the ultimate expressions of planting mania, of the desire to control nature to create a sympathetic and exciting environment, are mazes and labyrinths, which have roots deep in history and legend. In Christian terms they symbolize the soul's journey towards salvation; in their most primitive form mazes were simply traced out on the ground in stones or cut from turf; only later were they delineated by hedges. The gardens of the Villa d'Este boasted no less than four; in 1667 a maze was laid out in the highly symbolic gardens of Versailles around thirty-nine statues representing Aesop's *Fables*.

Perhaps the ultimate expression of the urge to control the planted environment was the turf amphitheatre. All over Europe these were modelled on those in Italian Renaissance gardens, particularly the one in the Boboli Gardens in Florence. The mania for control of the environment thus reached down to the earth itself and to the simplest of plants: grass.

Overleaf A design of the 1660s by Jean Le Pautre
for an elaborate parterre with a central pool and waterjet.

Florilegium Novum,
Hoc eſt:

VARIORUM MAXIMEQUE RARIO-
rum Florum ac Plantarum ſingularium unà cum
ſuis radicibus & cepis, Eicones diligenter ære ſculptæ
& ad vivum ut plurimum expreſſæ.

New Blumbuch
Darinnen allerhand ſchöne Blumen vnd frembde
Gewächs/ mit jhren Wurtzeln vnd Zwiebeln/
mehrer theils dem Leben nach in Kupffer
fleiſſig geſtochen/ zu ſehen ſeind.

Exhibitum nuperq̄ auctum.

A Iohanne Theodoro de Brÿ Ciue Oppenheimenſe. Aᵒ. M.D.CXII

Above The title-page of T. de Bry's *Florilegium*
of 1612, showing an ideal garden.

17

Frans gebouw, met cierlijke Parterres, etc.

B3

Opposite Detail of the moated garden of Jakob Trip, Alderman of Amsterdam. *c.* 1700.

Above Plan and bird's-eye view of a *parterre de broderie* garden with a revolving 'Holy Host'

fountain from *The Nether-landish Gardener* of 1699. **Preceding pages** A Dutch formal garden *c.* 1700.

Opposite and **above** Designs from *The Netherlandish Gardener* of knot gardens, planted with herbs and flowers and defined by small hedges of box or yew, and of a maze with a central tree.

Pages 22-23 This print of 1614 evokes the ideal garden of a Dutch couple, symbolic of the good life. **Pages 24-25** Typical Austrian Baroque garden, *c.* 1730: the symmetrical *parterres de broderie* are bordered with sculptures in the antique manner; the shrubs are clipped into the shape of cones and pyramids.

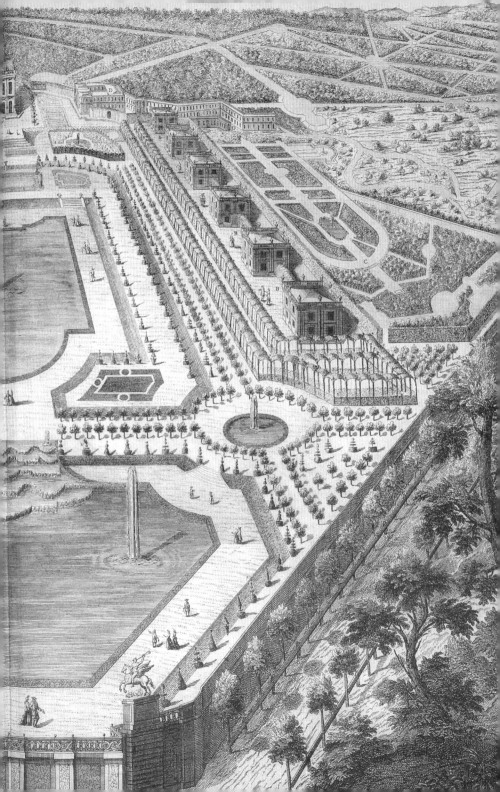

Above and **right** Two seventeenth-century Dutch gardens: the amphitheatre behind the manor at Assumberg: a country-house garden at Adrichem with similar features on a more modest scale.

Preceding pages Birds-eye view of the château and park at Marly. *c.* 1710, built near Paris by Louis XIV.

Opposite A plate from
Paul Decker's works (1711)
on the palaces of Prussia,
where he was Royal
Architect.

Above The Italian Baroque
gardens of Villa Pamphili
near Rome, from Piranesi's
Vedute di Roma (1740s).

Overleaf John Roque's 1738 view of a party
on the bowling green at Claremont, Surrey, England.

Above and **opposite** Two versions of the Baroque garden: the Governor's Palace.
Dominica; the Semplici Palace. Cisinello. Italy.

These pages Geometrical
forms for clipped shrubs
were popular from early
Renaissance times. These
ideas are from Colonna's

Hypnerotomachia Poliphili,
a philosophical treatise of
1499, in which the garden
becomes an emblem for
the expression of ideas.

Preceding pages Guiseppe Zocchi's view of the Castel' Pulci
in Tuscany as it appeared about 1740.

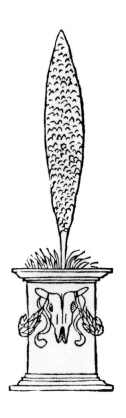

Overleaf Engraving by Nicolaus Visscher
of a late seventeenth-century German garden.

Below A garden from Paul Decker the Elder's early eighteenth-century volume on the palaces and parks near Berlin.

Opposite Part of a Dutch Baroque garden. with grotto. of the same period. recorded by Visscher.

A Paradise on Earth

45

Above A variation on the decorative 'bowling green' popular in the early eighteenth century, in the gardens of the Prince of Schwartzenburg, near Vienna.

Right Salomon Kleiner's view of a sunken 'bowling green', gardens of Count Althan, near Vienna.

Opposite and **below** The
renowned hedge labyrinth
of the Villa Pisani at Stà:
the gardens were designed
for the Venetian Doge
Alvise Pisani in 1735.

Above A mid eighteenth-
century engraving
of the renowned turf
'amphitheatre' at
Claremont, Surrey,
England. *c.* 1725.

Opposite An Arts and
Crafts interpretation of
a late Renaissance garden
by Thomas Mawson.

Preceding pages A proscenium arch of hedge frames
a view of the open-air theatre in a Dutch Baroque garden.

Opposite and **above**
Two spectacular avenues:
at Teddesley, seat of Lord
Hatherton, 1840s;

in the Vienna Angarten,
showing the Renaissance
and Baroque style of
clipping limes.

Overleaf A Dutch country-house garden. *c.* 1700.

These pages In the early seventeenth century many exotic and tender plants were imported from the New World. Learned botanical studies were produced with exquisite hand-painted illustrations. and writers gave information on the medicinal uses of the plants. with instructions for their care. These four

ALOË VERA VULGARIS.

ALOE FEROX.

kinds of aloes and a flowering cactus, from Abraham Muntinck's treatise, 1666, had probably never been seen before in Europe. Such plants would have been grown in forcing-houses.

Overleaf Empress Maria Theresa's gardens at the Favorita Palace.

Above The famous parterre terraces designed in 1851 by George Kennedy at Bowood, Wiltshire, in E. Adveno Brooke's contemporary watercolour.

Opposite Princely Baroque in the Netherlands: engraving by Nicolaus Visscher, 1709.

Preceding page The parterre gardens at Geubach, Austria.

Overleaf The Baroque water gardens at Geubach, Austria,
seat of the Counts Schönborn, 1728; by Salomon Kleiner.

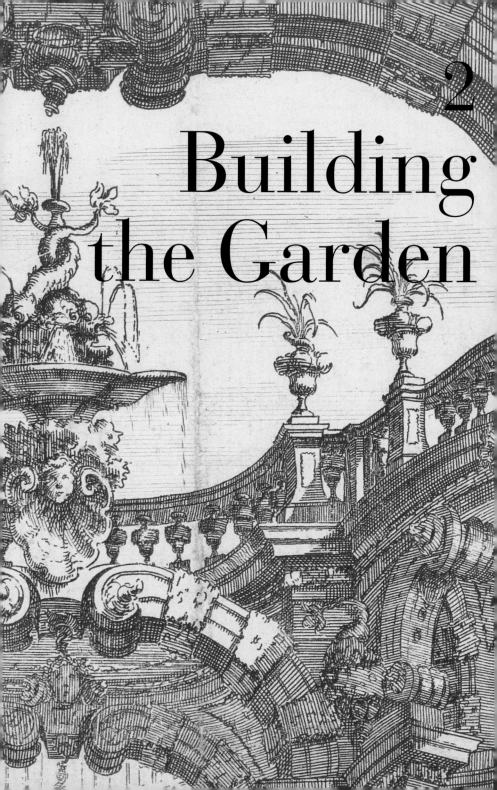

2

Building
the Garden

Temples of Delight

Garden buildings come in every shape, form and style and may serve every conceivable purpose: pavilions to rest in during the heat of the day, temples to draw the eye to the end of a vista, orangeries and conservatories to protect tender citrus plants during the winter and to provide shelter during foul weather, summer-houses for tea, and the family mausoleum, which may have its own special architectural attraction. Horace Walpole remarked of the mausoleum at Castle Howard in Yorkshire that it was enough to tempt one to be buried alive!

Buildings in gardens can make political and social points; at Stowe in Buckinghamshire, Lord Cobham mounted a sustained attack on the government of the day in his Temples of Ancient Virtue, Modern Virtue and British Worthies. They may display the wealth and culture of the owner, refer to the glories of Ancient Rome and the Italian Renaissance, or seek to emulate the extravagance of Versailles. Architecturally, they are often innovative and experimental. Many were never designed to be permanent and were demolished, moved or adapted to the latest whims of fashion

Opposite Detail from a High Baroque garden stage-set by Pietro Righini.

to which they were even more exposed than the house to which they were satellites. A severely classical temple for one generation could be transformed into a rustic grotto for the next. A Chinese house which had formed the central feature of a garden could be removed altogether within decades. For less illustrious patrons, architects like Batty Langley in the first half of the nineteenth century, and William Halfpenny a little later, produced pattern-books illustrating buildings in a delightful range of styles.

Garden architecture is an excellent indicator of prevailing fashions; grottoes, after their long and honourable history dating back to the nymphaeums of classical Rome, vanished without a trace before the wholesome Victorian distaste for damp and draughts. In their place, the summer-house and Swiss cottage became fashionable. The mass-production of glass and cast-iron in the nineteenth century brought a massive expansion in the use of greenhouses and conservatories and speeded the decline of the traditional orangery. Chinoiserie came and went, while the taste for all things Japanese flourished in the context of *fin-de-siècle* styles.

Paradoxically, although the garden is a place where plants normally flourish, it is frequently the buildings which shape and define this earthly paradise. The classicism of Palladio, the self-consciousness of the Picturesque, the real and fake medievalism of abbey, castle or folly, have all left their distinct marks on the spaces which both complement the main habitat and provide a counterbalance to it. Happy the garden owner of the late eighteenth century with a view of a genuine medieval ruin – abbey or castle – such as Fountains or Rievaulx. And if the real was lacking, then the fake would do very well, in the form of towers or hermitages, sometimes with a hermit in residence.

The forms of garden building are myriad: as well as more traditional types, they can include umbrellas, Turkish tents, viewing platforms, kiosks, bath-houses and let us not forget the architecture associated with the modern swimming-pool. As fashions come and go, so the importance of the illustrative print and pattern book becomes apparent, permitting glimpses of past building within the garden enclosure. The elaborate stone loggia of previous generations becomes the timber-decked roof terrace of today.

Above Section through
a garden pavilion near
Antwerp, Belgium, 1827.

Opposite A double-level
Belle Époque pavilion in
a German garden.

These pages Numerous
pattern-books were
published in the eighteenth
century of ideas for garden
buildings in every style:
here, Gothic, Hindoo,
Moorish and Classical.

Preceding pages The 'Fountain of Diana', an Italian Baroque extravaganza,
inspired by the gardens of Isola Bella, Lake Maggiore.

Compilations would
reproduce ideas and actual
designs from architects'
own publications,
disseminating styles
throughout Europe and
the colonies.

Garden Building.

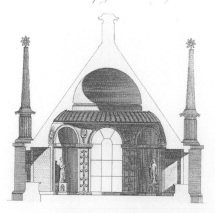

Section of Garden Building.

Opposite and **above**
Two Egyptian-style garden
buildings (possibly
mausoleums) with Classical
features, and a section of
a Moorish pavilion, from
the young Sir John Soane's
1797 *Designs in
Architecture*, an inventive
compilation of ideas for
temples and other small
decorative constructions
for the garden.

Overleaf A summer-house interior from Georges
Rémon's *La Décoration Intérieure*, Paris, c. 1895.

Opposite Engraving.
1784, of the Gothic Chapel
at Strawberry Hill,
Twickenham.

Above A mid-eighteenth-
century German design for
a Baroque garden temple
by J.J. Schübler.

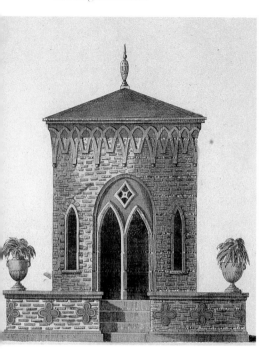

Opposite A tower-shaped pavilion with Gothic detailing: a Classical pavilion in the French style: and a domed bathhouse.

1802: the Gothic cottage (*top right*) design by Papworth was published in Ackermann's *Repository*. 1809–28.

Above Design by James Paine. *c.* 1770. for a Classical summer-house done in the Adam style.

Above A rustic 'Banqueting Room' from Charles Over's 1758 album of Gothic and Rococo garden designs.

Opposite Two designs for 'hermitages' from William Wrighte's *Grotesque Architecture, or Rural* *Amusements*, 1767. This book appeared at the height of the craze for Rococo.

Augustine Hermitage.

Pl.

Library.

Bath.

Winter *Hermitage*

Pl. 5.

Overleaf The 'Gloriette Chinoise' of the Prince
of Lichtenstein, near Vienna, 1790s.

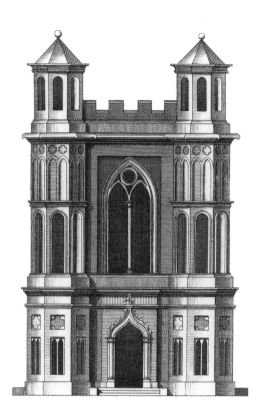

These pages Four eighteenth-century designs for garden buildings; the larger structures represent examples of Gothic-style pavilions, by Batty Langley (*above*) and by William Halfpenny (*opposite left*). The two Moorish temples *(above and opposite right)* are by Soane, reproduced in Le Rouge's survey of gardens.

Above A plate from Janscha's 1799 volume on the gardens of Hapsburg Austria: here, the Empress Maria Theresa's park at Laxenburg.

Opposite A design by Papworth for a Regency 'Garden Alcove' in Eastern and Chinese styles.

Overleaf The kiosk at Ranelagh, near Paris, from Le Rouge's *Jardins Anglo-Chinois*, 1784.

de Doorsnede van binnen te zien.

Riete dak.

A Dutch design for a 'rustic chapel' in the Adam style, 1802.

Opposite above Section
of a country house, 1827,
from an album of Dutch
and Belgian design.

Above A German design
for the interior of a 'Chinese
Garden Temple', 1779.

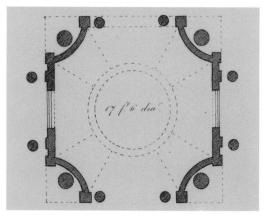

Above and **opposite** Two designs for garden temples from Soane's *Designs in Architecture*, 1778: a cuboid 'Temple for a Flower Garden' in Classical style, and a 'Rusticated Temple' with pillared porticoes.

Rusticated Temple

Overleaf A watercolour of a thatched 'hermitage',
Ackermann's *Repository*, *c*. 1820.

Banquetting House

Opposite and **above** Chinoiserie garden temples from Rococo pattern-books: Paul Decker's of 1759, with a detail; Charles Over's of 1758. Most such designs were too fanciful to be built.

Overleaf Design for an 'Imperial Angling Retreat', from Paul Decker's *Chinese Architecture, Civil and Ornamental.*

Above Baroque pavilions in the gardens of Prince Lichtenstein at Rossau. **Opposite** Façade of the 'Garden Pleasure House' at the seat of Count Althan: from Kleiner's survey of princely palaces in the vicinity of Vienna, early eighteenth century.

Above A two-storey
gardeners' cottage,
French, 1855.
Opposite Gardener's
house and greenhouse
from the same pattern-
book.

Overleaf A games room in Beaux-Arts style,
Nogent-sur-Mer, northern France, *c*. 1880.

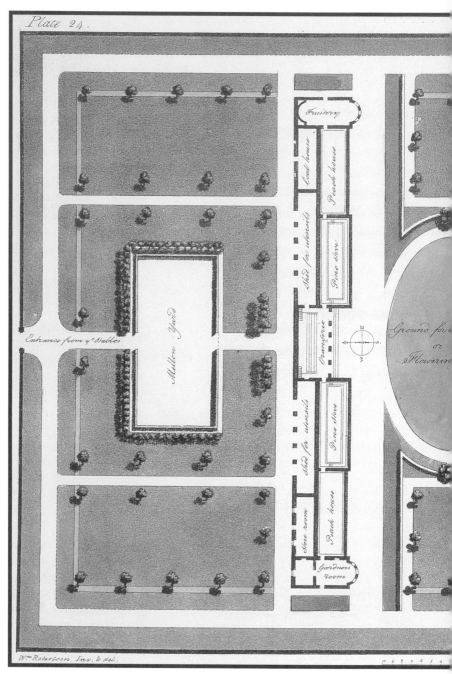

Plan by William Robertson, 1798,
for a range of 'stoves' or hothouses.

110

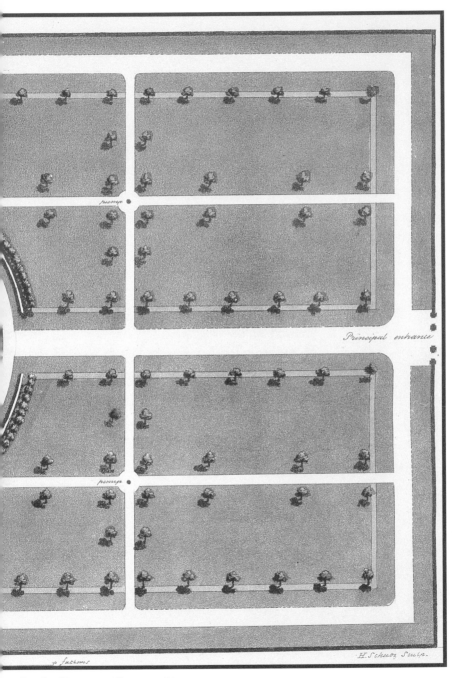

Principal entrance

pump

pump

30 fathoms

H. Schutz, Sculp.

Overleaf Sezincote, Gloucestershire,
built in 'Hindoo' or Indian style.

Above and **opposite** The
winter garden of the
Hofburg Palace in Vienna,
1852, richly planted with
tender plants and trees,
and serving as a popular
meeting-place for the
local gentry.

Overleaf Designs for Chinese-style pagodas by Le Rouge
and by Sir William Chambers, mid eighteenth century.

114

Tour
près de
Canton.

I.

117

Above The Chinese-style menagerie from Sir William Chambers' *The Garden and Buildings at Kew*, 1763.

Opposite A carved wooden pavilion in the Gothick taste, from Wallis's *Carpenter's Treasure*, c. 1793.

Preceding pages The Temple of Diana, Erlaw, Austria, with rocky cascade and Chinese bridge, late eighteenth century.

Above A Regency design for a bathhouse, with Greek, Egyptian and Oriental detailing.

Opposite Rusticated Classical façade for a mausoleum, Dutch, 1799.

Overleaf Engraving by Nicolaus Visscher of a Dutch
or German grotto, late seventeenth century.

Mausoleum for the P of Wales

Above Drawing, 1752, for a 'ruined mausoleum' by Sir William Chambers.

Opposite A 'ruined chapel as hermitage', from a Dutch pattern-book of 1799.

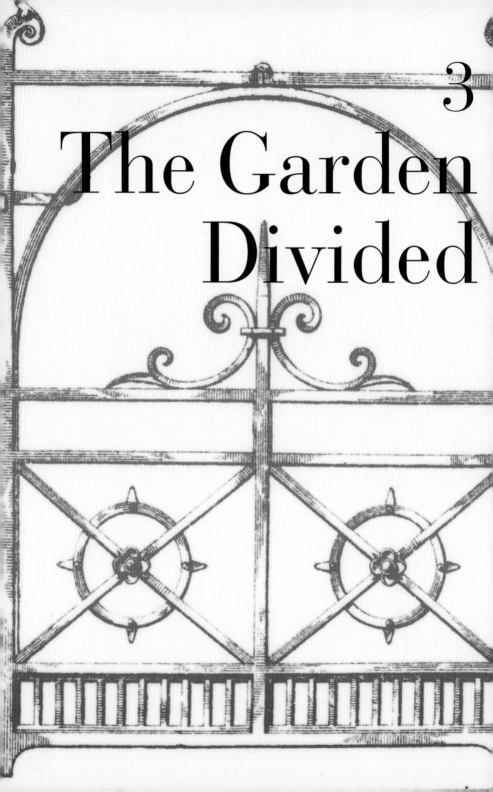

3

The Garden Divided

Gateways
and Enclosures

The garden is often a place of enclosures within an enclosure; its various parts can be imaginatively linked and divided in a delicious form of horticultural counterpointing. Bridges, terraces, steps, walls and pergolas provide, as it were, an armature for the whole area. In addition to their functional role, many such features are so elaborately conceived and decorated that they can be considered as ornaments in their own right. Bridges, for instance, may serve as crossings of expanses of ornamental water; yet their form, set off by the water itself, is all-important: classical or rustic, arched like Roman bridges, or covered like the wooden ones designed by Palladio in northern Italy. They can be made of wood, stone, brick, or even covered in turf. Bridges frame views or act as foci for the eye. They can be grand and Baroque, or as rustic as a simple plank of wood across a stream. They can be painted a brilliant lacquered red in the Oriental style to brighten up the dullest winter day, or left in their natural wood or stone to blend with their horticultural surroundings.

Opposite Cast-iron balustrading design, late nineteenth-century catalogue from Macfarlane's Castings.

Terraces, steps and staircases are the formal means of dividing and connecting different levels of the garden. By the middle of the seventeenth century monumental stairways and terraces were being put to dramatic use in Italian gardens to emphasize the hillside sites and, in theatrical manner, to link the architecture of the villa to the natural landscape. The gardens of northern Europe were less disposed to such grand flourishes, but occasionally a steep garden site allowed steps, terraces and balustrades to come into their own. At the beginning of the twentieth century the architect Edwin Lutyens created marvellously well-articulated gardens through the ingenious use of terraces and steps (almost always circular or curved) and other dividing and linking features – walls, alcoves, doorways and pergolas.

The construction of terraces and the steps or ramps to link them has now become prohibitively expensive; no modern gardener can easily undertake the movement of the colossal amounts of earth and rock to create the drama of soaring vertical elevation contrasting with horizontal perspectives of the great multi-level gardens. But we can still relish the art of the balustrade in gardens such as that of Isola Bella on Lake Maggiore. Seen from below, the balustrades delimiting the terraces seem to give the gardens an aerial aspect. And, looking from the gardens, between the cypress trees and decorative urns, they make a division between the finite, enclosed space of the terrace and the infinity of the lake and land beyond. On the subject of balustrades, Sir William Chambers wrote in 1759, 'Such as are intended for use… must always be nearly of the same height, never exceeding three feet and a half, nor ever being less than three. That is so a person of an ordinary size may, with ease, lean over them, without being in danger of falling.' He realized that the spaces between the balusters were important in relating the enclosed space to the openness beyond.

Yet, other delightful forms of division and opening remain for the present-day gardener. Walls, fences and hedges give privacy and shelter; the materials of their construction, the treatment of their tops, all offer opportunity for ornament and decoration. Gates and gateways – in closed or open work – give a perspective on other parts of the garden or serve to guard their secrets.

Pergolas were originally simple devices to support grape vines. Their decorative possibilities were fully developed by the end of the nineteenth century, until no self-respecting garden was complete without a lengthy run of such structures, with massive cross-beams of green oak supported on alternating square or round pillars. The heaviness of the overall structure was usually offset by cascading swags of rambling roses, clematis and honeysuckle.

The ultimate form of linking (and division, in a sense) has always been the elision of the perceived separation of the formal garden from the natural, semi-tamed lands around. Developed from military architecture, the ha-ha (the obscured sunken ditch) liberated the garden from any walls which limited it and launched it into the surrounding countryside. All Nature had become a garden and a means of return to Eden.

A view of the Chinese
pavilion and bridge, and
the House of Philosophy,
in the Parc de Bonnelles
near Paris, from Le Rouge's
Jardins Anglo-Chinois.

Above and **opposite**
Variations on the Chinese
bridge in eighteenth-
century European gardens,
as published by Le Rouge:
Windsor, Painshill, and
Attichi.

Above The garden at
Stourhead, Wiltshire,
now regarded as the iconic
Picturesque landscape
of Georgian England.

Opposite Even Robert
Adam designed follies: a
'ruined bridge' for Syon
House, engraved by
Vivares, 1768.

Overleaf The bridge across the Dell at Sezincote, Gloucestershire,
the 'Hindoo' house and garden designed by Thomas Daniell.

Opposite A design of
1822 for a single-arch
rustic bridge.

Above Chinoiserie bridge
with a central pavilion,
boat and viewing area,
Viennese, 1799.

Preceding pages Designs for garden bridges in Dutch and German pattern-books,
late eighteenth century and early nineteenth.

Opposite Design by
French Rococo architect
Gilles-Marie Oppenord
for a decorated arch.

Above A stagey design
of *c.* 1752 for a triumphal
arch by Pietro Righini.

Overleaf A massive arch in the winter garden of the Hofburg.
the former royal palace in Vienna.

Above 'Arcades for Piazzas',
from Batty Langley's
*Ancient Architecture
Restored and Improved...
in the Gothick Mode*, 1741.

Right 'Head of a Canal
or Termination of a Vista',
from Paul Decker's *Chinese
Architecture, Civil and
Ornamental*.

Overleaf A 'ruined temple with arch' in the gardens of Schönbrunn: from Janscha's 1790s watercolour.

Above A view from the
Upper Terrace at Shrubland,
Suffolk, a painting by
E. Adveno Brook.

Opposite This garden view
of Castle Coombe, Somerset,
also by Brook, combines
several styles – Gothic,
Classical and Baroque.

Preceding pages A seventeenth-century print by Abraham Bosse,
Paris, of a couple carrying blooms from the garden.

Opposite Seventeenth-
century designs by Jean
Le Pautre of wrought-iron
balustrading for garden
stairways.

Above The grand staircase
at the Villa d'Este, Tivoli,
from G.B. Falda's *Le
Fontane*, 1675–89.

Overleaf Double stairway linking the upper terrace and the lower
gardens of the Belvedere Palace, Vienna, 1720s.

157

Above and **opposite** German designs of 1775 for friezes; the garden of Jakob Schwind,
Mayor of Frankfurt-am-Main, engraved by Merian, 1641.

Above and **opposite** A straight path is the backbone of this formal garden design, *c.* 1900; in contrast, the path in the Picturesque garden winds circuitously.

Above and **opposite** These
treillage details are from
a garden recorded by Paul
Decker the Elder, architect
to the Prince of Prussia,
c. 1710; *treillage* would
commonly be covered
with greenery.

Preceding pages Alton Gardens in Staffordshire, built in the early
nineteenth century by the Earl of Shrewsbury.

Below and **right** Even simple walls may contribute to aesthetic effect, as shown in these two German gardens of the 1820s: a low wall of open brickwork, and the battlements of a terrace belvedere.

Opposite A trelliswork
pergola in the form of
a tower from a German
pattern-book of 1799.

Above A simple
trelliswork arcade from
Hypnerotomachia Polifili,
1499, recalling
a medieval garden.

Opposite Humphry
Repton's proposal of 1816
for an ironframe semi-
circular pergola at Valley
Field; fences and shutter
gates provide shade.
Above A painted or
whitewood single-frame
pergola support of the
1850s in the former royal
gardens of the Hofburg
Palace, Vienna.

Above A pair of cast-iron gates with spear-headed railings opening from a central spine, from an 1890s pattern-book.

Opposite A *clairvoyé*, or see-through screen, in the form of a wrought-iron gateway with grotesque decoration and set in a stonework arch, from Jean Le Pautre's 1660s pattern-book.

Above The gateway of a merchant's country house in the Low Countries, *c.* 1715.

Opposite The garden gates at Strawberry Hill, Horace Walpole's Gothic mansion, begun in 1751.

Overleaf A late nineteenth-century cast-iron gateway for the palace of the Maharajah of Kapurthala, by A. Marcel.

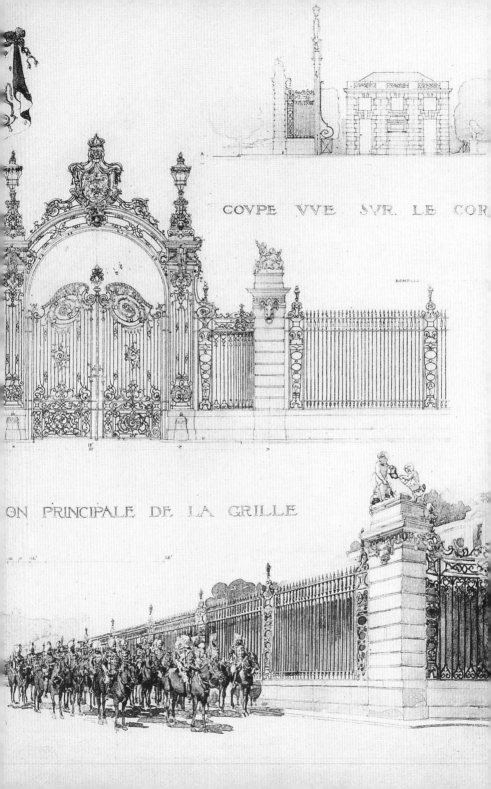

COVPE VVE SVR LE COR

ON PRINCIPALE DE LA GRILLE

ARDE   PLAN   GVERITE   CORPS DE

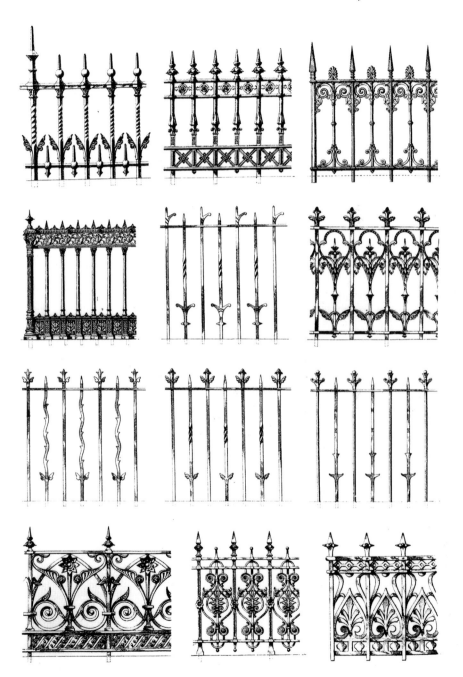

Opposite and **above** Designs for wrought-iron balconies by Jean Le Pautre, 1660s; nineteenth-century designs for cast-iron railings.

181

The simplest post and paling fence separates this
lodging house from its neighbour. 1825.

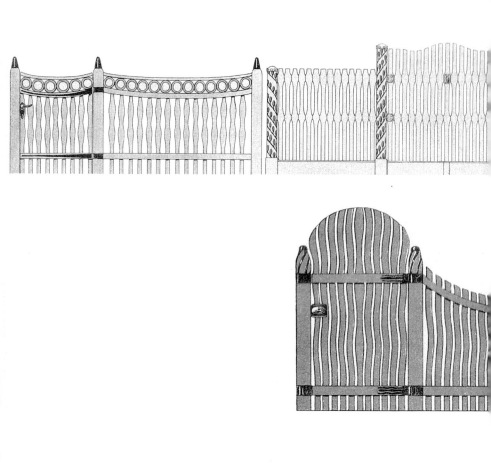

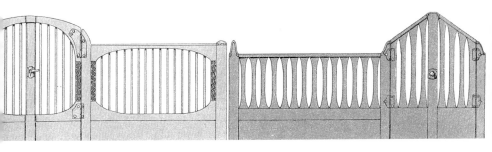

These pages Fences in Jugendstil, the German equivalent of Art Nouveau, by Gertrud Kleinhempel and Otto Bauriedl, published in *Documents: Architecture Moderne,* c. 1905.

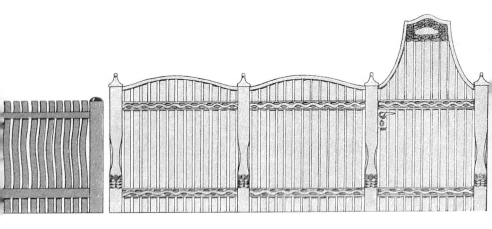

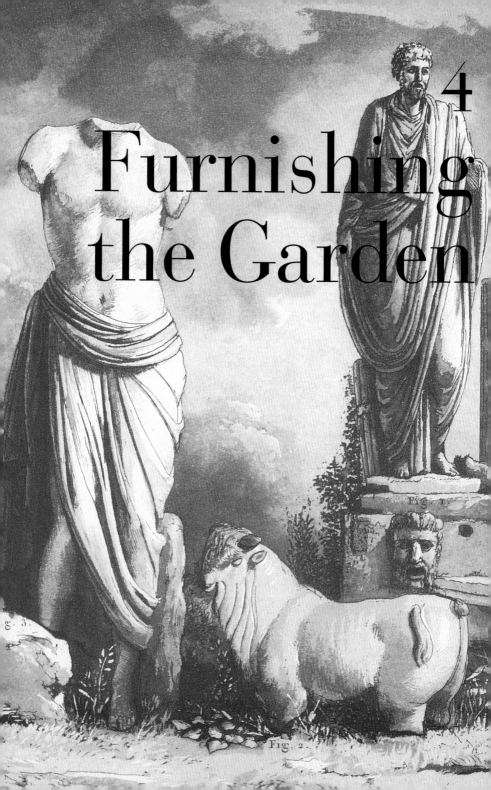

4

Furnishing the Garden

Ornament in Many Materials

Furniture is almost as essential to the fully realized garden as it is to the interior from which the garden is viewed. The setting may be beautiful and the architectural elements impressive, but seats and benches, statuary and urns undoubtedly add a fascinating dimension and embellishment to this paradise on earth. In medieval times, delight was taken in placing fountains in pools, creating turf benches on which to recline, and planting arbours with sweet-smelling climbing plants to give welcome shade on sunny days. Gilded heraldic beasts were placed on green and white striped poles throughout the garden to give a vertical dimension to what might have been an otherwise flat enclosure and, incidentally, to add lustre to a newly enriched family.

During the Renaissance and Baroque periods, the fashion for garden sculpture spread rapidly northwards from Italy, along with Italian craftsmen and architects. Soon, elaborate formal gardens throughout France, Germany and the Netherlands were richly adorned with gods and goddesses, nymphs, satyrs, shepherds,

Opposite Detail of excavated Greek sculpture fragments. *c.* 1813, from J.P.L. Houel's *Landscapes*.

shepherdesses and various beasts of the real and mythological worlds. Hercules, whose labours were reflected in the endless work required to maintain these formal gardens and who represented allegorically the traditional choice between virtue and vice, adorned gardens across Europe, not least in the monumental copy of the Farnese Hercules which dominates the garden at Vaux-le-Vicomte in France. Gilded statues in the gardens at Peterhof outside St. Petersburg catch the rays of the sun and add a golden splendour to the magnificent setting.

At Versailles, apart from the charming set of sculptures illustrating Aesop's *Fables* in the maze, the groups of figures designed by Charles Le Brun reflect the image of Louis XIV as the Sun King. Apollo, the god of the Sun, rises from the waters at the end of the canal. His mother Latona stands surrounded by villagers metamorphosing into frogs, while elsewhere sculptures and fountains reflect the hours, days and seasons as they are governed by the sun.

The materials of garden furniture have always reflected fashion; they have also reflected climate. Marble predominated in Italy, but could not stand the effects of northern winters. Local stone could be harder wearing and cheaper. In England, Portland stone was the most highly prized for sculpture. Cheapest of all materials was lead, sometimes painted in bright colours or made to resemble stone, a sort of poor man's marble. Lead statuary and urns were popular from the late seventeenth century onwards. Gates, railings, seats and benches were usually made of wrought-iron, often with wonderful craftsmanship.

The Industrial Revolution brought new materials to garden ornament. The comparative delicacy of wrought-iron was supplanted by the intricate heaviness of cast-iron, which was cheaper to produce in bulk. The Coalbrookdale and Britannia Ironworks dominated much of international nineteenth-century production, turning out fern-leaved seats and ranges of urns, vases and other sculptural items. The French foundries were noted for their production of animal figures. Bronze, though expensive, is hardwearing and ideally suited to garden use; it was almost exclusive to the Continent, particularly France. Artificial stone was introduced as a material for garden ornament from the 1760s onwards; stone and then cement were used as the base materials. Mass-produced from moulds, garden ornament spread to a much wider market during the nineteenth and twentieth centuries, as the desire to own a small piece of the classical past spread from grand gardens to much more modest plots.

Above and **opposite** Two
examples of circular seats
from Charles Over's 1758
pattern-book. *Ornamental
Architecture.*

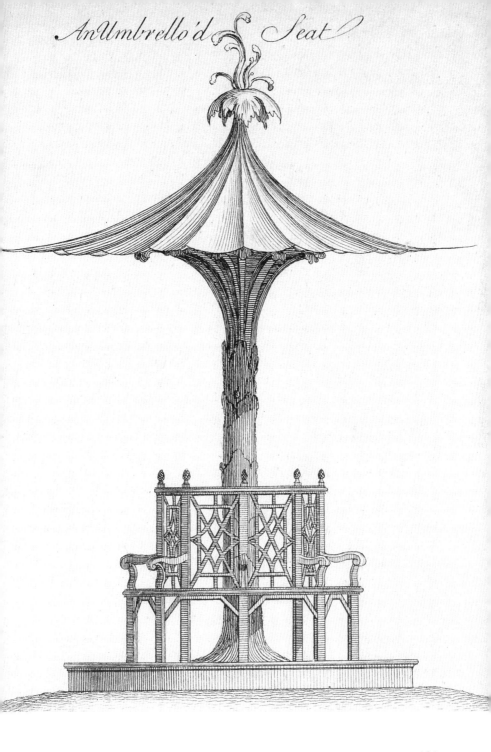

An Umbrello'd Seat

Opposite Two designs
by Papworth from *Rural
Residences* for tented
umbrella seats, of a kind
very popular in Regency
England.

Above A terminal seat in
Classical style from a Dutch
pattern-book of 1802.

Preceding pages C.R.
Ashbee's designs for green-
stained wooden garden
terrace furniture in Arts
and Crafts style.

Above An ingenious Gothic-
style garden building
combining a grotto seat for
reading and relaxation,
with a tented gazebo above.

Opposite Two ladies
exchange confidences
on a French green-stained
garden bench, print by
Carmontelle.

Overleaf A selection of chairs and benches for the garden,
from William Wrighte's *Grotesque Architecture*, 1768.

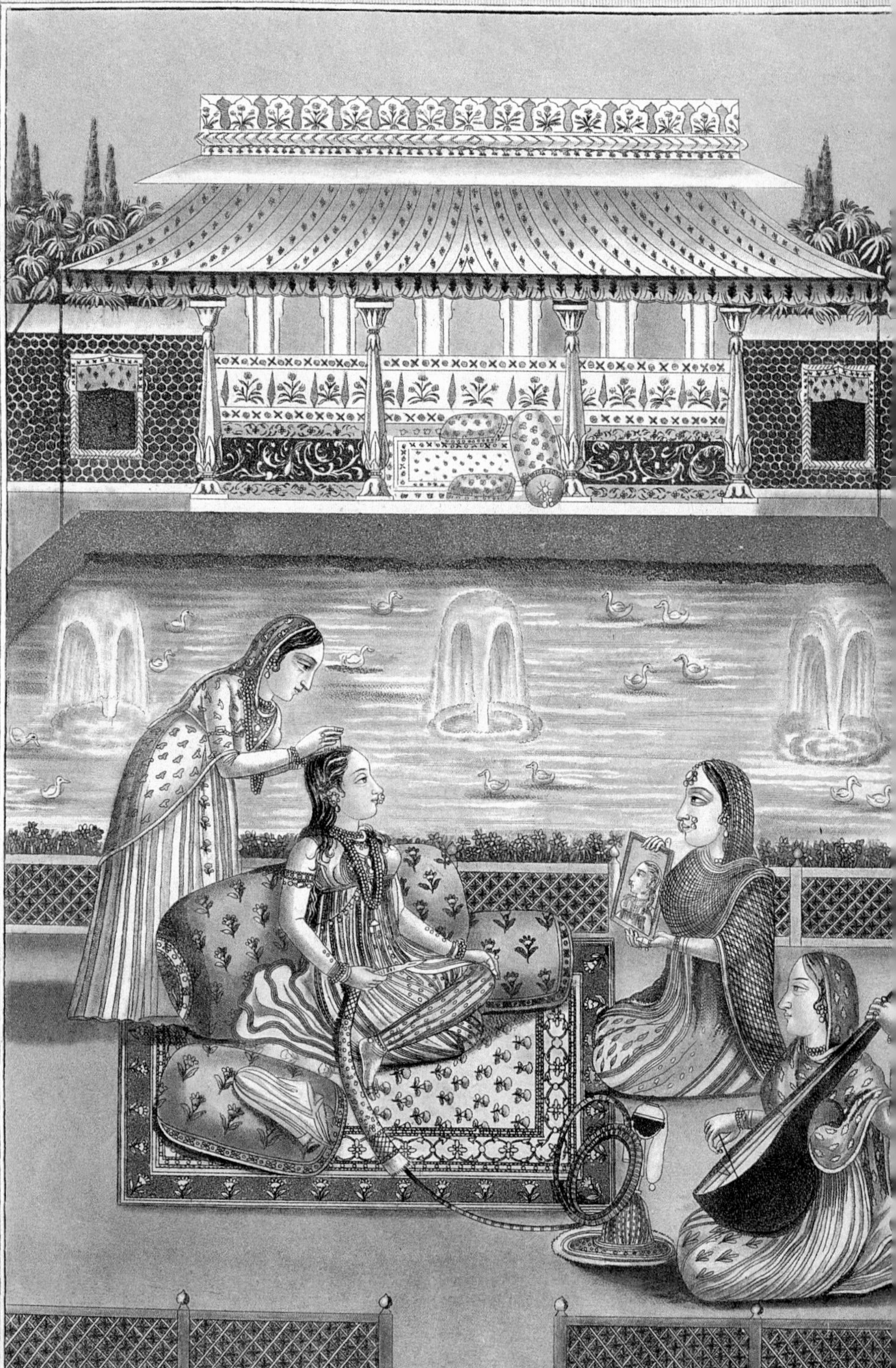

Opposite and **above** A classical Mughal garden tent
and two contemporary versions.

Alcove Seat.

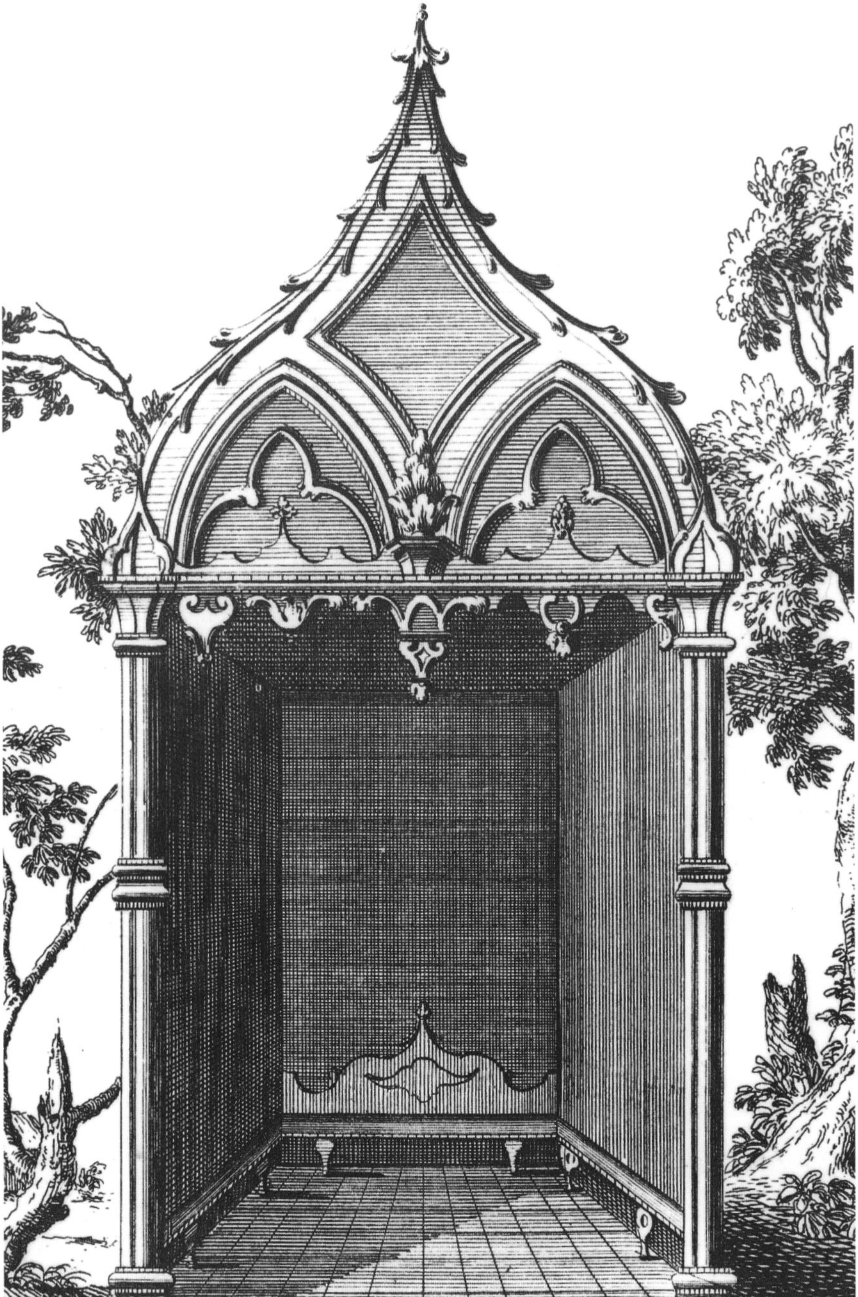

Opposite Design by Paul Decker for a wooden seat in the Gothic style.

Above French design for a stone bench with scrollwork supports set against an architectural wall, 1880s.

Above Two designs for planters for the conservatory by the Regency cabinet-maker George Smith.

Opposite A nineteenth-century French planter from *Album de l'Industrie et des Arts Utiles.*

Above Dutch design for a
table and chair carved from
tree-trunks, *c.* 1802.

Opposite Three pier-tables
for summer-houses from
William Wrighte's *Grotesque
Architecture*, 1768.

Preceding pages Diners on a terrace: a seventeenth-century
print by Moncornet: note the elegant wine-cooler.

Above and **opposite** Two loggias from Jean Boussard's survey of garden buildings in northern France, *c.* 1880:

a pavilion on simple pine supports, and a flat-roofed loggia with square column supports.

Preceding pages The 'Rustic Seat' at Shrubland, a famous Italianate Suffolk garden.

Above and **opposite**
Variations on the arbour:
an Austrian garden shelter
of trunks supporting a
thatch roof, and a cast-iron

arching frame for flowering
climbers, designed
for Charles Barry's
mid-Victorian gardens
at Trentham Hall.

Above and **opposite**
Loggia-style summer-
houses in Regency times
ranged from rustic thatched
'cottages' to classical
elegance.

Overleaf A Chinoiserie textile design of an imaginary garden,
with curving pergola and central archway.

Above Bronze urns, from
designs for the gardens
of Versailles, 1664–89,
probably by Claude Ballin.

Opposite A German design,
c. 1735, of an urn for citrus
trees, by Martin Engelbrecht.

Above In the 1820s the gardens of Wilton were redesigned in the fashionable Anglo-Italian manner.

Opposite An Anglo-Italian style flowering urn in the terrace gardens at Woburn. redesigned by Repton during the Regency.

Above Classic terracotta
pots planted with *cereus
minimus* and *hepatica
trifolia*, painted by G.D.
Ehret, *c.* 1745.

Opposite A clipped bay
tree in a square wooden
tub with ball feet and
finials, still a common sight
on contemporary terraces.

225

Above A watercolour design by Sir William Chambers for a massive neoclassical urn.

Opposite Three eighteenth-century Dutch designs for garden urns by engraver Simon Schynvoet.

Above and **opposite** Herms would typically be used in Renaissance gardens to line avenues; these examples from an account of Versailles. late 1600s. show Mercury. Minerva. Apollo. and Daphne.

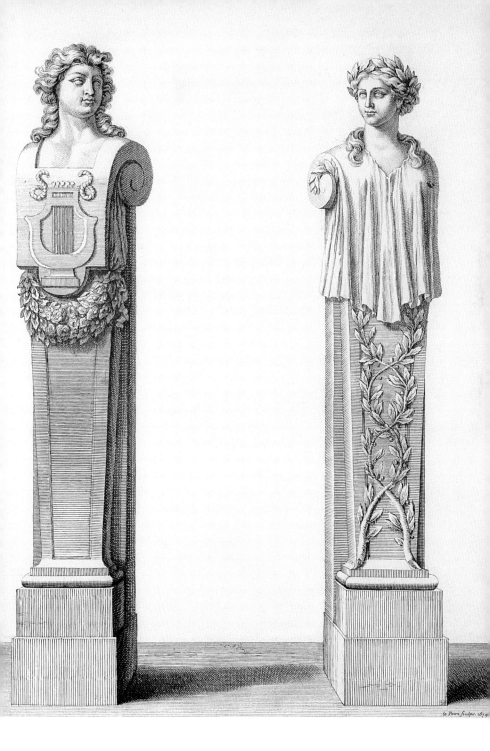

le Povre sculps. 1674

229

Above Detail from an engraving. *c.* 1729, of the orange-tree garden at Chiswick House.

Opposite Frontispiece to Mondon's volumes of Rococo designs for garden architecture. 1736–49,

showing artists at work in an imaginary ruin.

Overleaf One of Galli da Bibiena's Baroque designs of *c.* 1740 for entertainments and operas in a garden setting.

Opposite and **above** Two colossal statues of satyrs which decorated the *allées* in the 'wilderness' beyond the *bocage* at Versailles.

Opposite and **above**
Designs for marble sphinxes
mounted by playful gilded
bronze *amours*, or *putti*, on
raised stone bases decorated
with carved swags:
engravings from a volume
on Versailles of the 1690s.

Overleaf Setting for a Baroque opera in a splendid garden filled
with tiers of statues after the antique.

Overleaf The nineteenth-century rose garden at Nuneham Courtney.
with cupid statues on pedestals.

Opposite The frontispiece
from Antoine Le Pautre's
Les Œuvres d'Architecture,
c. 1651.

Above Gentlemen converse,
improbably perched in a
Rococo shell seat on a wall,
design by Jean Mondon.

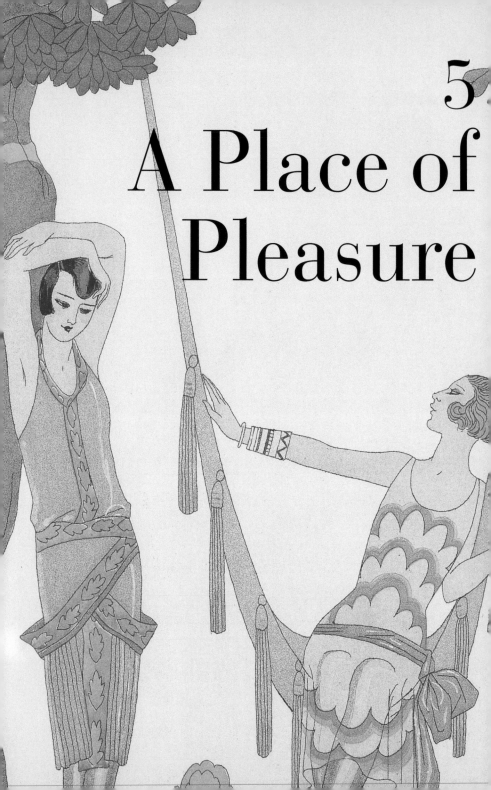

5

A Place of
Pleasure

Amusements and Entertainments

The words 'pleasure garden' may conjure up images of the *louche* night-time delights of Vauxhall Gardens in eighteenth-century London, but pleasure and amusement have often been part of the private garden too. While great cities had vast spaces to entertain the fashionable public with players and orchestras, moonlit concerts, alfresco eating, fireworks and romantic adventures, more secluded and personal places have been enlivened with embellishments simply to delight, from swings and see-saws to the modern swimming-pool. The Chinese pagodas, Turkish tents, Moorish temples and Swiss cottages which were scattered in profusion throughout the gardens at Vauxhall have their equivalent in the tennis-courts of contemporary suburbia.

The spirit of Rococo frivolity in the mid eighteenth century, especially, brought a flavour of casual relaxation to the garden. Devices such as swings and see-saws provided amusement and a measure of sexual *frisson* as billowing skirts revealed momentarily more leg than modesty approved. In France, the gardens at Ram-

Opposite Conversation piece on the garden swing: fashion plate from the *Gazette du Bon Ton*, 1920s.

bouillet were notable for their gigantic and elaborate constructions devoted entirely to play. At Marly, the Duchesse de Bourgogne was famously entertained by 'La Roulette', a gilded toboggan on rails, which the Duchesse and her ladies could ride with happy abandon down a steep incline towards the château. The same spirit of exhilaration made a fashion out of the 'Montagne Russe', or sliding hill; artificial slopes for sledge or toboggan rides had originated in Russia as mounds built out of snow and ice. By the nineteenth century, the helter-skelter had become a standard attraction in fairgrounds and parks.

Formal games, too, have always been an essential part of life in the garden, public and private. *Mail*, an early version of 'golf', was played at Marly in the seventeenth century, while Pall Mall in London acquired its name from the game of *paille-maille*, a form of croquet. Bowling greens were an almost standard feature of seventeenth-century English gardens, and archery remained popular until the nineteenth century.

One of the principal contributions of modern times to the numerous delights of the garden has undoubtedly been the swimming-pool, though garden bathing had been in fashion in earlier times. In the Middle Ages, mixed bathing was a quite acceptable form of relaxation. In later centuries immersion in water came to be regarded with the deepest suspicion; by the eighteenth century, bathing was considered therapeutic, rather than pleasurable. Cold plunges were built in the form of stern, Spartan, stone-edged pools, fed by springs and planted thickly around with evergreens to give year-round shade. The swimming-pool, as we generally know it, is a twentieth-century invention, deriving its popularity originally from the French and, particularly, German cult of sun-bathing in the 1920s. One of the first organically shaped pools was designed by Thomas Church in 1947 at El Novillero, Sonoma, California. Its kidney shape was later much derided as being vulgar and ostentatious, but the architect considered it would integrate more naturally with the flowing natural lines of the garden.

Menageries to house wild animals have been popular since ancient times and were an established feature in Roman gardens. An elaborate example was built at Versailles, in the form of an octagonal pavilion in the centre of an octagonal courtyard, enclosed with wrought-iron screens. It housed birds as well as animals, which included two elephants, camels, ostriches, flamingos and penguins. Fifty years earlier, James I of England had built his own menagerie in St. James's Park. There was also a menagerie in the park of Schönbrunn in Vienna, built in 1752, and another at the Jardin des Plantes in Paris, dating from 1794.

Perhaps the peak of the garden as a place of entertainment was reached at Versailles in the seventeenth and eighteenth centuries, when the park became the setting for entertainments and fêtes to mark gala occasions. In Louis XIV's reign plays and masques by Molière and Racine, with music composed by Lully, were performed in temporary theatres that encompassed large areas of garden. The canal was illuminated and ships and palaces floated on it, while make-believe monsters rose from the depths. The garden theatre of the Sun King, as a place of celebration and frivolity, has never really been surpassed.

Above The swing at Rambouillet, near Paris, operated by ropes and pulleys.

Opposite A somewhat nervous lady in a chair swing, early nineteenth-century French fashion print by Delacourt.

Les Parisiennes à Montmorency.

Le Bon Genre, N° 41.

Above A chair swing beneath a cherry tree, *c.* 1810, from the *Bon Genre* series.

Opposite A very basic swing, from a French fashion plate of the 1920s.

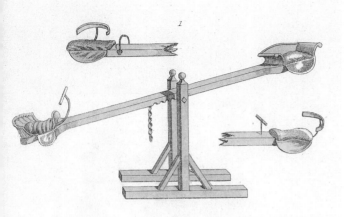

Above A wooden see-saw, from a Dutch pattern-book of 1802.

Below Designs for swings on arch frames from the same book.

Opposite A swinging seat beneath a 'Chinese' tent roof, 1799.

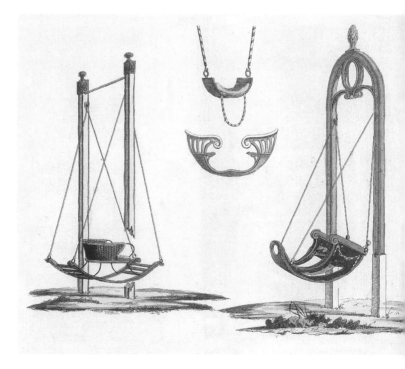

Overleaf An early nineteenth-century print after L. Garneray of the 'Montagne Russe' (Russian Mountain), a helter-skelter in a Paris park.

Above A German design, *c*. 1800, for a miniature carousel or whirligig with bucket seats for two girls and cantilevered extensions for more adventurous boys. **Opposite** A basic wood-frame ferris wheel with wicker-work seats, worked by pulleys on a wheel and ratchet system, *c*. 1800.

Opposite A belvedere with deck surround and steps attached.
Below A thatched open- fronted arbour shelter; both examples are from Victor Petit's *Habitations Champêtres, c.* 1855.

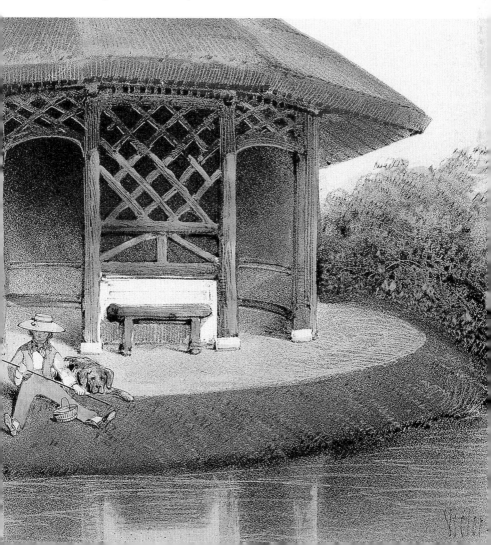

Above and **opposite** Two designs for rustic pavilions beside water by Victor Petit: one shelter serves as boathouse and landing stage, while the half-timbered pavilion with a six-gabled roof makes an attractive belvedere.

Above High Rococo – the boating lake facing the 'Egyptian' belvedere at Steinfort, as published by Le Rouge, with chain ferry in Chinese style and a 'Cantonese' junk.
Opposite A gondola-style punt with a Chinese canopy.

Above The swimming habit from the *Gazette du Bon Ton*, 1913.

Opposite A convenient topiary half-*clairvoyé* provides a glimpse of these flappers' summer dip, from *Galérie des Modes*, 1920s.

Above and **opposite**
Renaissance and Baroque
garden designers often
provided amusements in the
form of joke fountains:
typically, water would spurt
forth to soak the passer-by,
activated by foot pressure or
other devices; these two
examples are from Falda's
Le Fontane.

Overleaf A party from a riverside house takes to the ice in a horse-drawn
gondola sleigh, engraving by Lannesin after Watteau's *Winter*.

A boy guides his sleigh with his brother and their nurse, early eighteenth-century German print.

Above Thomas Mawson
designed this 1909 cricket
pavilion for Thornton
Manor in Westmoreland.

Opposite Pavilions for the
practice firing-ranges built
at La Favorita, a royal
palace near Vienna,

recorded by Salomon
Kleiner, 1720s.

Above Garden skittles, from a German pattern-book of 1799; framework and enclosure are in Gothic style.

Opposite An ornamental swing slung between two sculpted figures, in high Rococo Chinoiserie style,

from Le Rouge's *Jardins Anglo-Chinois*.

Above and **opposite**
Observatories in the form
of belvederes and gazebos
embellished many a well-
furnished eighteenth- and
nineteenth-century garden:
two fine 1850s examples
from France in Victor
Petit's rustic manner.

Overleaf A mid-eighteenth-century group scans the surrounding countryside
with a telescope, while gentlemen try their luck in the fishpond.

276

Above A gazebo with
a stairway in its central
column offers views of
the lake in the park of St.
Denis, Paris, 1880s.

Opposite A French hostess
waves from her terrace; a
plate from the *Gazette du
Bon Ton*, 1913.

Overleaf A garden building in the bastion walls of a French country house; the doors
below give access to steam baths, from Boussard's survey, *c.* 1880.

280

MACHINE · · VAPEUR

Above and **opposite** Plates
from the *Gazette du Bon
Ton* showing guests at a
private entertainment, and
a woman descending a flight
of steps into the garden
– to keep a tryst?

Overleaf A night-time entertainment amid the *treillage* of the Salon at Versailles in the reign of the Sun King.

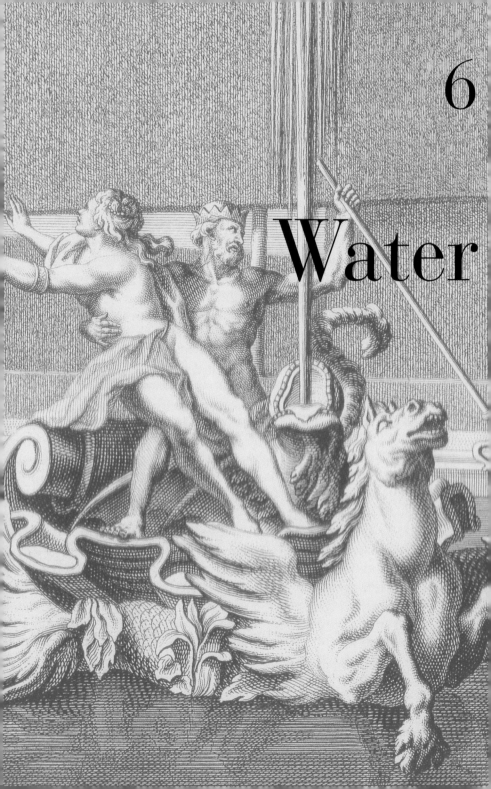

6

Water

The Most Vital Element

Water brings life to gardens; without it, all plants would die. Yet water is more than just sustenance: its flash and sparkle as it falls in a cascade or its chatter as it runs down a hill or staircase delights the eye and soothes the ear. Water in the garden has the property to exhilarate, even to alarm, but it may also bring peace and inward calm. From the very earliest times gardeners have manipulated the element to achieve a myriad of effects.

Moving water excites: fountains, rills and cascades all raise the spirits. These special qualities were fully understood by the designers of Mughal and Islamic gardens. Water chutes of carved and fretted marble were angled to catch the sun, creating a reflection from the sparkling water as it fell from one terrace to another. At night-time, candles were placed behind cascades to give glittering illumination. In Italy, the water which pours from the Oval Fountain at the Villa d'Este delights in its richness and complexity, while at Caserta the onlooker is overawed by the monumental cascade which runs towards the palace. The French designers and gardeners of Versailles and Vaux-le-Vicomte made sure that their magnificent fountains were overwhelming in their number and variety. And in the great gardens of Peterhof, near St. Petersburg, the water cascades into marble basins and is then shot skywards from gilded figures, before running into a canal which stretches towards the Gulf of Finland in the distance.

The mechanical properties of water have also been harnessed to enliven the garden. In the great Baroque gardens of Italy hydraulic pressure activated automata to surprise and alarm – birds sang, organs played and concealed jets soaked the unwary guest. In more modem times water has been used to create screens to conceal bathers in swimming pools or to veil sculptures, a device inspired by Indian Mughal gardens.

Still water is calming and refreshing. Islamic gardens contained tanks of water, full to the brim to reflect the surrounding architectural glories. Gertrude Jekyll, the great Arts and Crafts gardener, was influenced by memories of the Alhambra; Sir Edwin Lutyens created Moorish tanks with covered walks on two sides. At Versailles, the Parterre d'Eau immediately outside the garden front of the palace is composed of two large mirrors of water in which the elaborate façade of the palace is reflected. The canals of so many Dutch and Dutch-inspired gardens have the same effect of inducing feelings of peace and tranquillity.

Water in movement and standing water were combined with marvellous ingenuity in the gardens of the English Landscape Movement of the eighteenth century. Natural-seeming lakes were created over several acres; reflected in their still waters might be a temple or an urn on an island, or perhaps a grotto. The water could then be directed to plunge over a spectacular cascade into a further lake, creating drama and excitement to equal that of the most architectural Italian garden. At Chatsworth, in Derbyshire, the canal to the south of the house, dug at the command of the first Duke of Devonshire when he decided to have a hill which blocked his view removed, reflects the house, which seems to rise up from the mirror of the water. And, then, water in dramatic movements erupts, as a gardener opens a valve with a giant key and the jet from the Emperor Fountain rises thirty metres into the air. The image in the mirror is shattered.

LES III. FONTAINES.

Opposite The fountains at Versailles were Louis XIV's favourite feature: Dominic Girard, author of this 1714 engraving,

was chief fountain engineer.
Above The 'Spirit of Valour', centrepiece of a Versailles fountain, *c.* 1670.

Above and **opposite** Two
engravings of *rocaille* Cupid
fountains from the series
of 1670s volumes on

Versailles: scallop shells.
cupids. dolphins. and lyres
were favourite motifs
of the period.

Above and **opposite** The labyrinth of *bocage* with *treillage* arbours at Versailles was ornamented with small fountains on the theme of Aesop's *Fables*: in 1770 these were recorded by Daniel Bellamy Snr. in his volume of *Ethic Amusements*.

Above left Detail of the
Fountain of Venus at
Versailles, by Girard.

Above right A Rococo
fountain design by Jean
Mondon the Younger.

Opposite Design for a
Baroque fountain in the
'Italian style' by Jean Le
Pautre, Paris, *c.* 1661.

Preceding pages The double Terrace of One Hundred Fountains cuts across the main axis
of the Villa d'Este, Tivoli, from Falda's *Le Fontane*.

The circular lake at
Versailles was a popular
meeting-place for the
courtiers of Louis XV.

Above and **opposite** Sea
gods and aquatic creatures
– strange fish and dolphins
– were common motifs in
fountain design in both
the 17th and 18th centuries;
the fashion started in the
Baroque period.

304

Opposite Three designs for
revolving fountains, to be
set in the centre of a pool.

from *The Netherlandish
Gardener*, 1699.

Above The goddess
Arethusa in an ideal
garden, *c*. 1736.

Overleaf The 'Rustic Fountain' on the cascade at the Villa
Aldobrandini, Frascati, from Falda's *Le Fontane*.

Font d'Arebuſe

PARTIE HAUTE DE LA RIVIERE.

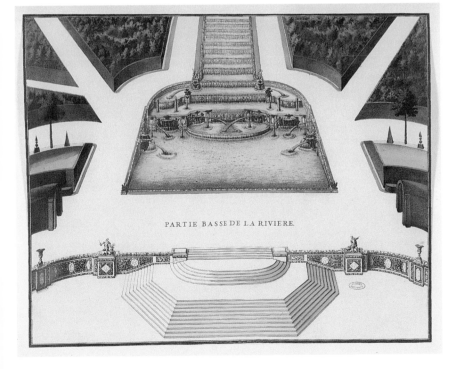

PARTIE BASSE DE LA RIVIERE.

Preceding pages Details of the plans of the water features at the Château de Marly.

Above and **opposite** The Picturesque use of water in eighteenth-century English parks: the ornamental lake with cascade at West

Wycombe, engraving by Woolett, 1757; the waterfall at Bolton Park, Lord Burlington's Yorkshire estate.

Overleaf The symbolic channelling of water in the Islamic garden: engraving of Babar's Tomb, Atkinson's *Afghanistan*, 1842.

Below and **opposite** Two
cascades by D. Girard for
Le Nôtre's 'theatre of water'
at Versailles; the Great
Cascade was set in an
amphitheatre.

317

Opposite Sightseers at the Fountain of Diana and Apollo, from *Plans, Profils de Versailles, c.* 1715.

Above The Fountain of Poseidon and Thetis at the Belvedere Palace, Vienna, from Kleiner's 1730s work;

the sea-nymph Thetis, beloved of Zeus and Poseidon, was the mother of Achilles.

Preceding pages The lake at Stourhead was intended to represent Lake Avernus, across which Aeneas sailed to Hades; watercolour, *c.* 1780, by W.C. Bamfylde.

Water

Left A formal pool fronting the Pavilion at Brighton, from Repton's 1808 book, engraved by Stadeler and presented as a gift to the Prince Regent.

Above The Grand Canal at Fontainebleau, engraved by I. Tinney, 1794; canals, a device of the Dutch formal garden, were enthusiastically adopted by the French.

Above A round lily pond
with brick edging and crazy
paving: a French design
of the 1920s.

Right Pool with onion
dome pavilions, roofed
loggia and arcaded alley,
from Repton's Brighton
Red Book, 1808.

Preceding pages The pool at Sezincote, with the temple to
the Hindu sun-god Souriya: etching, *c*. 1817, by John Martin.

326

Above Stowe landscape
garden, *c.* 1752, with the
river and grotto.

Right Detail of an 1890s
plan by Thomas Mawson
for Lord Lever's garden in
Westmoreland.

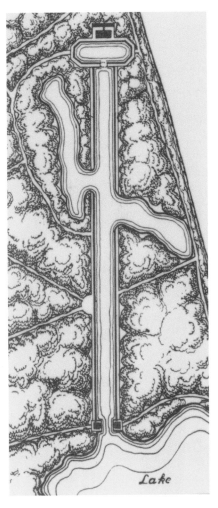

Lake

Above The Fountain Court
of the Alhambra, palace
of the Moorish kings
of Granada.

Opposite The Alhambra's
Court of the Lions, bisected
by a rill.

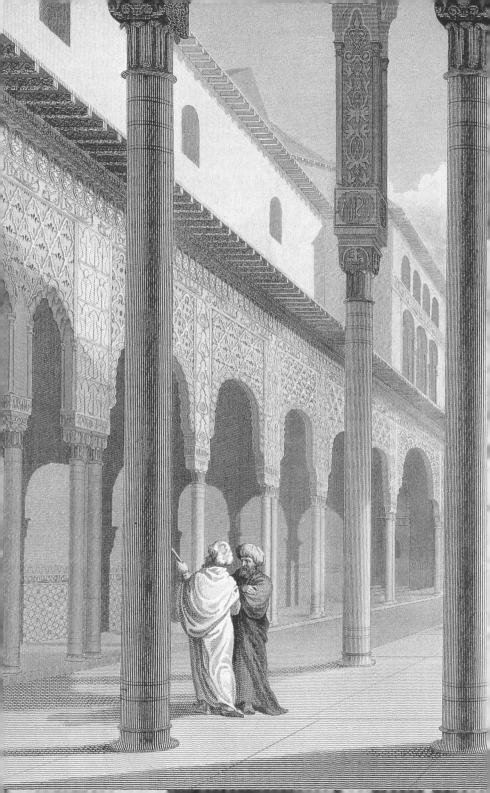

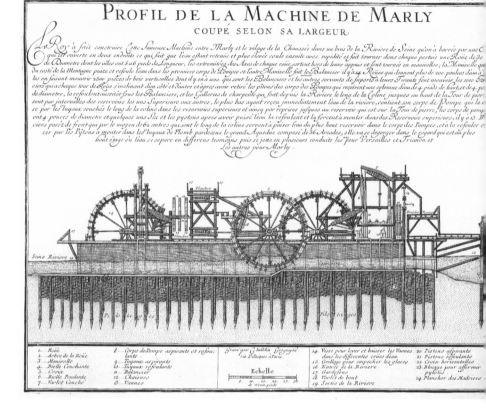

Above This machine at Marly was installed to lift water from the river to service other features of the park.

Opposite Water pump and well-head fountain. operated by two Moorish servants. early eighteenth-century engraving by Jacob Schübler.

Preceding pages Through the canopy to the Court and Fountain of the Lions at the Alhambra. engraved by S. Porter after J.C. Murray. 1815.

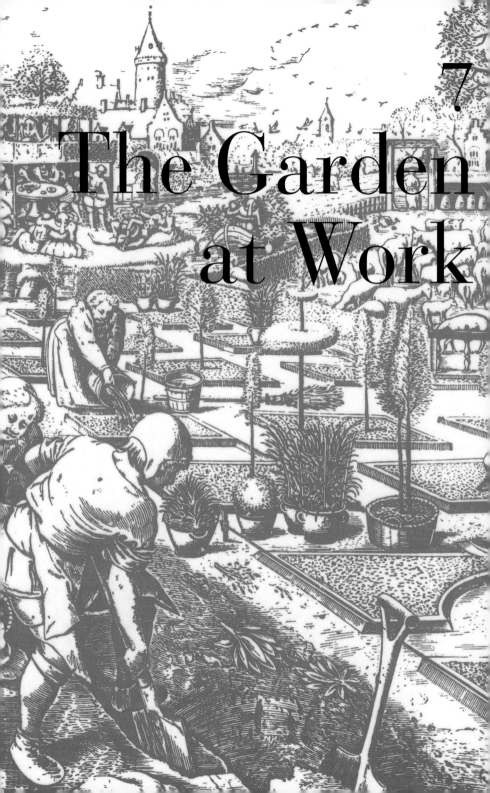

7

The Garden
at Work

Providing and Protecting

The working garden is both the reverse and the complement of the pleasure garden; it is the practical and functional area where vegetables and fruit are grown for the table, where bees are kept, birds reared for the pot, fresh-water fish kept in ponds, where clothes are dried and herbs grown for cooking and sweetening the air. While often seen as the quintessential expression of nineteenth-century gardening, the walled kitchen garden, or *potager*, goes back in concept to the very origins of gardening. Even the Ancient Egyptians, though keen ornamental gardeners, employed nurserymen for the mundane work of growing flowers and herbs for medicines, cooking and cosmetics.

In the Middle Ages a stream of herbals extolled the growing of vines, herbs and other practical plants, while ornament was relegated to a secondary role. Vine husbandry was especially significant; even England was known as a producer of dry white wine, much of which was exported to the Continent. Indeed, vineyards continued to be an important part of large working gardens in Western Europe until the beginning of the eighteenth century. In

Opposite Detail from an engraving. *c.* 1570, by Pieter Breughel the Elder of a family of gardeners.

France, the simple *potager* was occasionally elevated to great heights of sophistication; the Potager du Roi at Versailles, under the direction of Jean de la Quintinie, author of *Instructions pour le jardin fruitier et potager*, inspired a revival of decorative kitchen gardens, where ornamental vegetables and flowers grew side-by-side with others of more practical application. De la Quintinie was also required to provide a constant supply of cut flowers for the palace throughout the year; at the Grand Trianon the garden was filled with tender, sweet-smelling flowers, grown and forced under glass by an army of gardeners.

Over the centuries the kitchen garden underwent much improvement. It was walled to keep animal pests at bay; later, flues were built within the walls to create 'hot walls' to aid the cultivation of peaches and apricots and other frost-susceptible fruits. 'Crinkle-crankle' walls were built in a zig-zag pattern to catch and concentrate sunlight for the same purpose. Gardeners had always recognized the importance of winter heat in the cultivation of citrus fruits and other exotics, but only gradually was the importance of light understood. Unfortunately, the elegance of earlier buildings, such as graceful eighteenth-century orangeries, with their long windows and high arched doors, disappeared with the coming of the Industrial Revolution, which made possible great palaces of sheet glass and iron, as well as mass-produced suburban conservatories.

From its hey-day in the nineteenth century, when seed-merchant's lists were studied as avidly as catalogues for tools and gadgets, from bill-hooks to lawnmowers (invented by a Mr Budding in 1832), the kitchen garden went into gradual decline, as labour costs rose and gardens were simplified or, even worse, built over. In the past two decades or so, however, there has been something of a revival of the working garden, fuelled partly by fashion and partly by the growing demand for fruit and vegetables grown without the use of insecticides or herbicides: twenty-first century gardening embraces sixteenth-century methods.

Overleaf The great orangery of the Belvedere Palace, Vienna, *c.* 1728, is dismantled for the summer.

Above and **opposite** Two
plates from G.B. Ferrari's
Hesperides, an account
published in 1646 of

Cardinal Pio's botanical
gardens at the Villa
Aldobrandini: terraced
hothouses with the roofs

removed for summer; a
vaulted forcing-house with
lattice screens and shutters.

ALDOBRANDINORVM
CELLA TVSCVLANA
TVTANDIS PER HIEMEM
AVRANTIIS

Above and **opposite** Jan Commelyn's Dutch adaptation of Ferrari's *Hesperides* for a colder climate, 1676: trees are moved into the garden for the summer; the family visits the forcing-house with dogs.

345

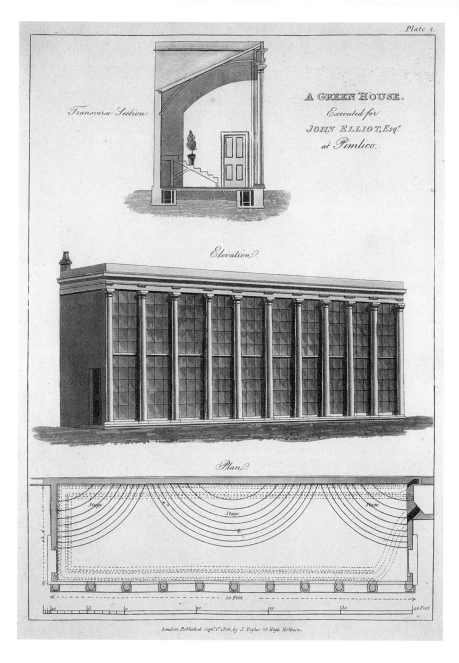

Plate 2.

Transverse Section.

A GREEN HOUSE.

Executed for

JOHN ELLIOT, Esq.

at Pimlico.

Elevation.

Plan.

Stage

Stage

Stage

50 Feet

40 Feet

London, Published Sept.r 1.st 1806, by J. Taylor 59 High Holborn.

Above and **opposite** George Tod published his book of greenhouse designs in 1812: classical design for a London townhouse: a simpler design for a provincial home.

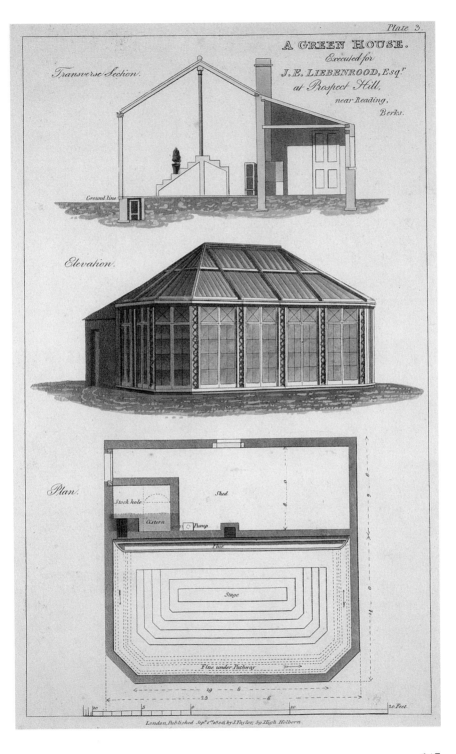

Green-house.

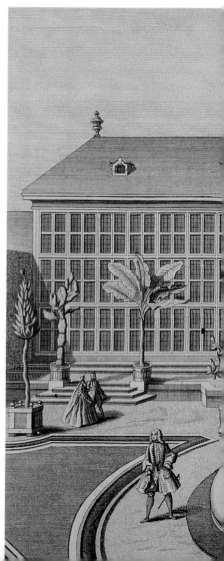

Pl. 28.

Opposite A gabled cottage-style greenhouse faced with *rocaille* decoration, by William Wrighte, 1760s.

Below The façade of the great forcing-house of the Belvedere Palace, Vienna, 1720s.

Opposite and **above**
Designs from George Tod's
1812 book: two sections
showing the interiors, one
with a stepped stand for
pots, and the other showing
the method of training
peach trees and vines; two
views of a small greenhouse
supported on stilts to
adjoin the sitting-room
of a London house.

Overleaf A range of greenhouses at the Cambridge Botanical Gardens,
from Ackermann's 1815 *History of Cambridge*.

Above A page from
Repton's 1808 *Red Book*
for Brighton Pavilion shows
a gardener transplanting
pot-raised rose bushes in
to a fretwork trough.
Opposite A design of 1818
by Papworth for a 'Gothic
Greenhouse'.

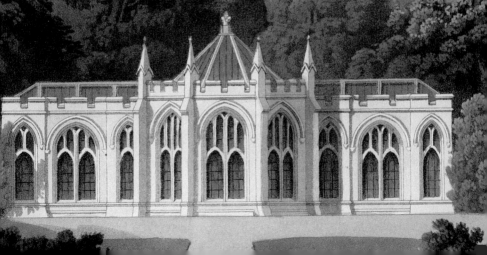

In this charming print
of 1780 three ladies visit
the potting shed, probably
to choose plants for the
house or conservatory.

357

Opposite and **below** Plates from the 1616 translation of Crispian Van Der Passe's *Hortus Floridus*, published at the height of 'tulipomania': a metal contraption for extracting tulips from the ground; wire holders to keep them erect.

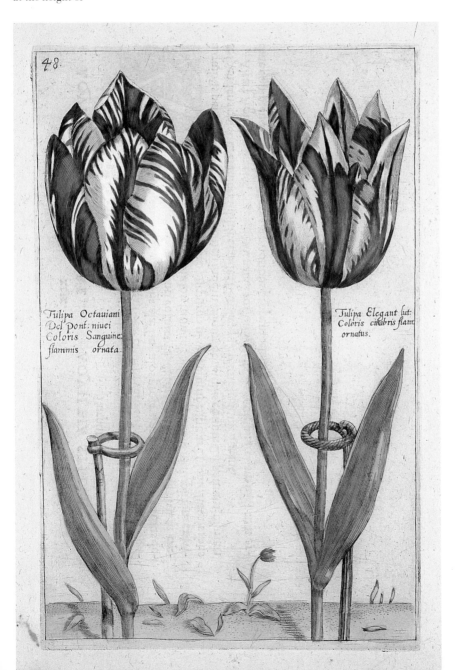

Above A diagram published
c. 1905, showing the
layering of new vines from
a single root.

Opposite The grafting,
pruning and training
of vines, from Commelyn's
1676 version of Ferrari's
Hesperides.

Het inleggen der Wijngaerden.

Oculatie der Boomen.

Opposite and **below** Two
plates from Commelyn's
Hesperides: grafting
for fruit trees, and the start
of training for an espalier.

Het af-Zuÿgen der Boomen.

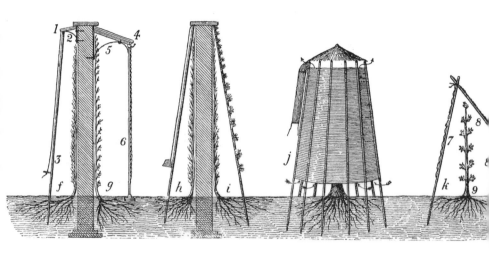

Above Protecting blossom from frost, for both free-standing and wall-trained trees, from *The Fruit Grower's Guide*, c. 1905.

Opposite Symbolic planting of a tree, a common motif for the frontispiece of early gardening manuals; from *The Retir'd Gardener*, 1706, by George London and Henry Wise.

Above Designs for
wheelbarrows and a tray;
from *The Fruit Grower's
Guide*.

Opposite A selection of
tools for pruning fruit trees,
from Ferrari's *Hesperides*.

Overleaf 'Cultivators'
from Diderot's *Encyclopédie
des Sciences et des Métiers*,
1751–72.

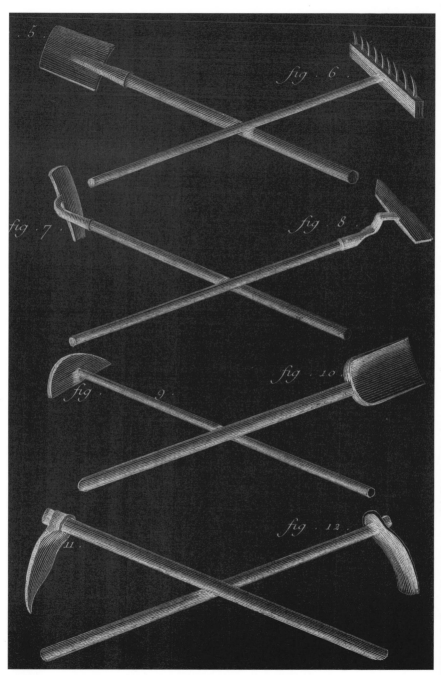

Opposite A French fashion print of the 1920s shows a girl leaning on an improbably heavy-headed spade.

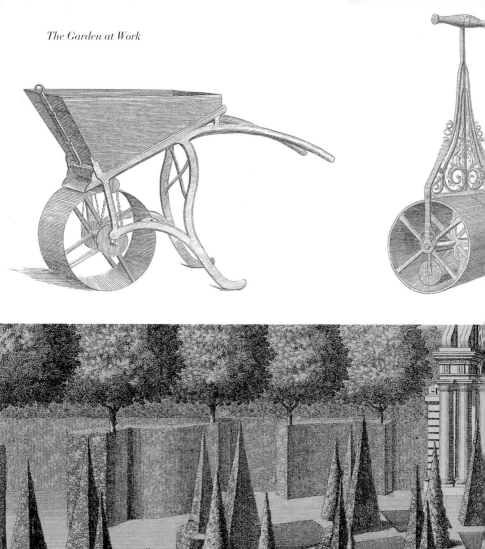

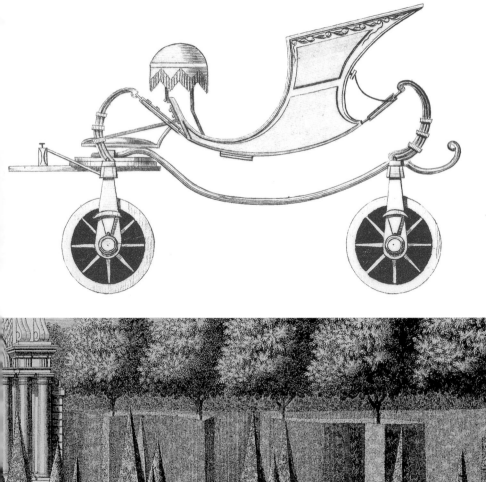

Preceding pages Moving citrus trees in a Viennese Baroque garden.

Above The frontispiece to Ferrari's *Hesperides*, on citrus trees, Italy, 1646.

Opposite The title-page of, Abraham Muntink's 1666 'Accurate Description of Earth-Crops'.

Pages 370–1 Scaffold platform-ladders for pruning, Schwartzenberg Palace, Austria.

NAUWKEURIGE
BESCHRYVING
DER
AARD-GEWASSEN,
DOOR
ABRAHAM MUNTING.

T. Utrecht by FRANÇOIS HALMA,
Te Leiden by PIETER VANDER AA, Boekverkoopers.
MDCXCVI.

Above Useful aids for
the gardener from Diderot's
Encyclopédie: wood screen,
seed-scatterer, watering cans.

Opposite Frontispiece
to Repton's 1808 *Red Book*
for the Brighton Pavilion,
including tools for
construction and garden
maintenance.

FLORA

Cherishing
WINTER

GARDENS

ARE WORKS OF ART

RATHER THAN OF NATURE

DESIGNS THAT ARE VAST
ONLY BY THEIR DIMENSIONS, ARE ALWAYS
THE SIGN OF A COMMON AND LOW IMAGINATION:
NO WORK OF ART CAN BE GREAT BVT AS IT DECEIVES;
TO BE OTHERWISE IS THE PREROGATIVE OF
NATVRE ONLY.

BURKE on the Sublime &c.

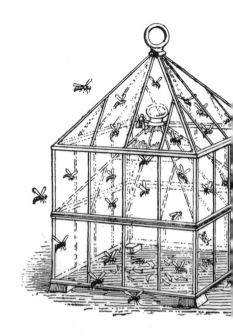

Above and **opposite** Three
methods of dealing with
insects, from *The Fruit
Grower's Guide*, c. 1905.

Opposite A ladder-scaffold on wheels for pruning mature trees.

Above A hand-drawn open-backed cart to remove prunings and other debris; both illustrations are from Diderot's *Encyclopédie*.

Overleaf Tools from Johann Van Der Groen's *The Netherlandish Gardener* (1699), one of the earliest and most influential gardening manuals.

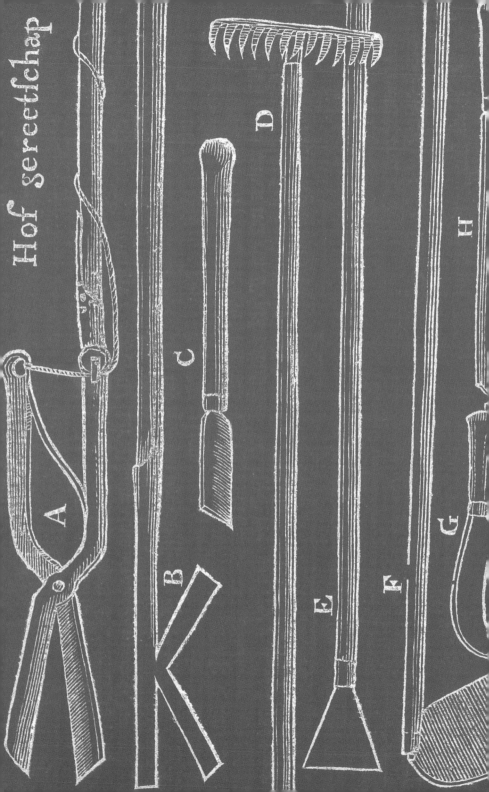

Hof gereetſchap

A

B

C

D

E

F

G

H

K

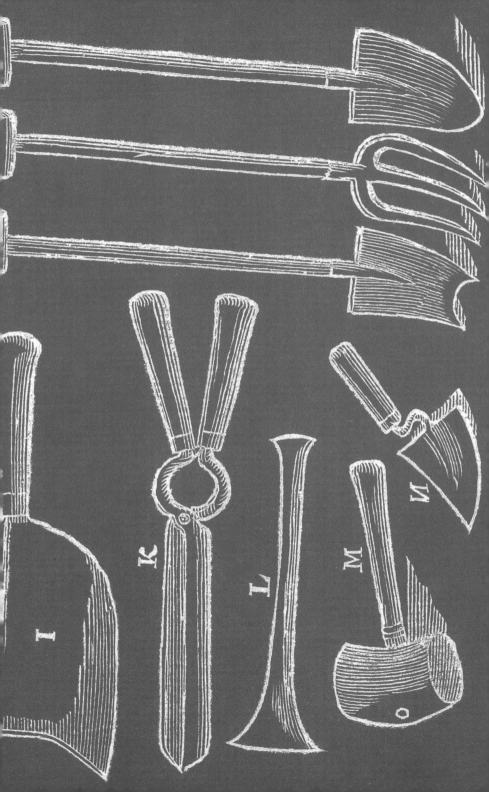

Above Victor Petit's 1855
French icehouse is insulated
with thatch down to the
ground.

Opposite Papworth's
Regency icehouse takes the
form of a solid Neo-Greek
mausoleum.

Opposite A wrought-iron
aviary surmounted
by a gazebo.

Left A 'shelter for volatiles'.

Above A shelter for
waterfowl; all designs
from Jean Boussard's
collection, *c*.1880.

Above The aviary at Kew
Gardens, built by Sir
William Chambers in 1763,
engraving after Paul Sandby.

Opposite Repton's
design for the pheasantry
at Brighton Pavilion.

PROJET D'UN PIGEONNIER
*pour Madame la Duchesse
de la Tremoille a Attichi
par Bellini*

Opposite A pagoda design for a pigeon loft, recorded by Le Rouge in his *Jardins Anglo-Chinois*, 1770s.

Below A rabbitry, *c.* 1660s, at the Villa Barbarigo, Italy, by D. Rossetti, 1702.

Opposite Interior
and exterior of an apiary,
from an 1802 Dutch
pattern-book.

Above Papworth's design
of 1822 for an apiary,
in bee-stripe colours.

Overleaf Sir John Soane's thatched dairy
at Hamels in Hertfordshire.

BIBLIOGRAPHY

(page nos. refer to reproductions in this book)

Ackermann, Rudolf, *History of Cambridge*, 1815 *350*

Ackermann's Repository, 1809–28 (chromolithographs) *98/99*

E. Adveno Brooke, *The Gardens of England*, 1857 (chromolithographs) *2, 54, 62, 154, 155, 164/5, 210/1, 215, 222, 223, 242/3*

Atkinson's Afghanistan, 1842 (watercolours by Louis-Charles Hague) *314/5*

Bellamy, Daniel Snr., *Ethic Amusements*, 1770 *296/7*

Boussard, Jean, *Constructions et Décorations pour Jardins. Kiosques - Orangeries - Volières - Abris divers*, c.1880 (work of various architects, drawn & engr. by Boussard) *108/9, 203, 212, 213, 280, 282/3, 386, 387*

Chambers, Sir William, *The Garden and Buildings at Kew in Surry*, 1763 *120, 388*

Cierney, L., *Garden of the Hofburg Palace, Vienna*, 1852 *114, 115, 146, 173*

Collection of New Ideas for the Garden, c.1799 *75, 95, 140, 170, 196, 252, 253, 256, 263, 274*

Colonna, Francesco (attrib.) *Hypnerotomachia Poliphili* ('The Strife of Love in a Dream'), 1499 *40, 41, 171*

Commelyn, Jan *De Nederlandze Hesperides*, 1676 *344, 345, 361, 362, 363*

De Bry, J. Theodore, *Florilegium Renovatum...* (inc. *Der Garten des Burgermeisters Schwind*), 1641 (drawn & engr. by Matteus Merian) *17, 161*

Decker, Paul, the Elder, *Fürstlicher Baumeister, oder: Architectura Civilis*, 1711, 1713, 1716 *32, 44, 45, 166, 167*

Decker, Paul, the Younger, *Europae Speculum*, c.1736 *307*

Decker, Paul, *Gothic Architecture Decorated*, 1759 *202*

Decker, Paul, *Chinese Architecture, Civil and Ornamental*, 1759 *100, 102/3, 149*

De Leth, Hendrick & Brouerius Van Nidek, Mattheus, *Het Zegenpralent Kennemerlant, vertoont in veele Heerelyke...Gezichten ven deszelfs voornemeste Lust- plaetzen, Adelyke Huizen, Dorp- em Stede-Gebowen*, c.1700–30 *18/19, 266, 267, 289, 303, 308/9*

Diderot, Denis, *Encyclopédie des Sciences et des Métiers*, 1751–72 *368, 376, 380, 381*

Documents: Architecture Moderne, Vol. I, c.1900 *184/5, 194/5*

Duncker, Alexander (pub.): *Die Landlichsen Wohnsitze, Schlösser, und Residenzen des Ritterschaftlichen Grundbesitzen in der Preussischen Monarchie*, 1852/63 (lithographs after watercolours by T. Hennicke) *168, 169*

Ehret, G.D.. (albums of botanical drawings), 17th century *58/59, 224*

Engelbrecht, Martin, Suite of Designs for Vases, fl.1730–55 *9, 10, 221*

Egan, Pierce, *Life of an Actor*, 1825 *182/3*

Falda, Gio. Battista: *Le Fontane di Roma, Parts I-IV*, 1675 – c. 1690 (drawn/engr. by Falda, Venturini & Fantetti) *157, 266, 267, 298/9, 303,308/9*

Ferrari, Giovanni Battista, *Hesperides*, 1646 *342, 343, 367, 374*

The Fruit Grower's Guide, c. 1905 *360, 364, 366, 378/9*

Galérie des Modes, late 18th century *1, 6, 249, 250*

Galli da Bibiena, Giuseppe, *Architetture e Prospettive*, 1740 (engrs. by Andrea Pfeffel) *232/3, 238/9*

Gazette Illustrée des Amis de Jardins, 1825–27 *310/311*

Gazette du Bon Ton, 1913 and 1920 *244, 251, 264, 265, 281, 285, 369*

Goetghebuer, Pierre-Jacques, *Choix des Monuments, Édifices et Maisons les plus remarquables du Royaume des Pays-Bas*, 1827 *70, 94*

Halfpenny, William, *New Designs for Chinese Temples*, 1752 *88*

Hofland, Mrs T.C., *Descriptive Account of the Mansion and Garden of White Knights*, 1819 *216/7*

Houel, Jean-Pierre-Louis, *Landscapes*, c. 1813 *186*

Janscha, L., *Public Parks and Gardens in the Vicinity of Vienna*, 1799 (engrs. by Johann Ziegler) *55, 86/87, 90, 118, 119, 142/3, 150/1, 214*

Kleiner, Salomon, *Vorstellung beyder Schlösser Weissenstein ob Pommersfeld und Geubach*, 1728 *61, 64/65*

Kleiner, Salomon, *Vorstellungen… folgender Lustgärten ausser der Residenz-Stadt Wien*, c. 1728 *24/25, 47, 60, 104, 105, 225, 273, 370, 372/3*

Kleiner, Salomon, *Résidences memorables… Édifices et Jardins de Prince Eugène-François, Duc de Savoye*, 1731–40 *158/9, 288, 321, 340/1, 349*

Langley, Batty & Thomas, *Ancient Architecture Restored and Improved*, 1741-42 (later re-issued as *Gothick Architecture*) *88, 148*

Le Bouteiller, *Album de l'Industrie et des Arts Utiles*, 19th century *205*

Le Pautre, Antoine, *Les Œuvres d'Architecture*, 3rd ed. (first with text), 1652 *240*

Le Pautre, Jean, *Œuvres*, c. 1661 *4, 16, 156, 175, 180, 301, 304*

Le Rouge, Georges-Louis, *Jardins Anglo-Chinois: Détails des Nouveaux Jardins à la Mode*, 1770–87 *52, 88, 89, 92/93, 117, 132/3, 134/5, 248, 262, 275, 390*

London, George, & Wise, Henry, *The Retir'd Gardener*, 1706 *365*

Macfarlane's Castings (trade catalogue), c. 1890 *128, 174, 181*

Marcel, Alexandre, *Compositions Décoratives et Architecturales*, 1895–1920 *178/9*

Mariette, Jean, *L'Architecture Française* (vol. on Versailles and Marly), 1738 *334*

Martin, John, *Views of Sezincote House*, c.1818 (set of aquatints in sepia by F.C. Lewis after etchings by Martin) *112/3, 138/9, 324/5*

Mawson, Thomas H., *The Art and Craft of Garden Making*, 1900 *53, 162, 329*

Mawson, Thomas H., *Civic Art: Studies in Town Planning, Parks, Boulevards and Open Spaces*, 1911 *272*

Mondon, Jean, *Livre de Formes Rocailles et Cartels*, in 6 vols. 2 series, 1736 and 1749 *231, 241, 300*

Muntinck, Abraham, *Naauwkeurige Beschryving der Aard-Gewassen* ('Accurate Description of Earth-Crops'), 1666 *375*

Oppenordt, Gilles-Marie, *Oeuvre… contenant différents fragments d'architecture et d'ornements…*, 3 series as 1 volume, c. 1745 *144, 305*

Over, Charles, *Ornamental Architecture in the Gothic, Chinese and Modern Taste*, 1758 *84, 101, 190, 191*

Paine, James, *Plans, Elevations and Sections of Noblemen's and Gentlemen's Houses*, 2 vols. 1768 and 1783 *83*

Papworth, John Buonarotti, *Rural Residences, consisting of a series of designs for cottages, small villas, and other ornamental buildings…*, 1818 *82, 192, 355, 384*

Papworth, John Buonarotti, *Hints on Ornamental Gardening, consisting of a Series of Designs for Garden Buildings*, 1823 *91, 122, 142, 393*

Pein, Georg, (fl. 1775) *Ideen zur aussern und innern Verzierung die Gebäuden* (Ideas for the Decoration of Buildings), *160*

Petit, Victor, *Habitations Champêtres, Receuil de Maisons, Villas, Chalets, Pavillons, Kiosques, Parcs, et Jardins*, c. 1855 (chromolithographs) *106, 107, 258, 259, 260, 261, 276, 277, 384*

Piranesi, Giovanni Battista, *Raccolte di varie Vedute di Roma si antica che moderna*, c. 1740–50 *33*

Rémon, Georges, *La Décoration Intérieure*, Paris, c.1900 *78/79*

Repton, Humphry, *Designs for the Pavilion at Brighton*, 1808 *322, 327, 354, 377, 389*

Repton, Humphry, *Fragments on the Theory and Practice of Landscape Gardening*, 1816 *172*

Rigaud, Jacques, *Receuils… des Palais Châteaux et Maisons Royales de Paris et des Environs*, 1730 *302*

Righini, Pietro, *Theatrical Variations*, c. 1742 *67, 145*

Robertson, William, *A Collection of Various Forms of Stoves*, 1798 *110/1*

Rossetti, D., *Le Fabbriche e i Giardini dell'Ecc. Casa Barbarigo a Valsansibio*, 1702 *391*

Schübler, Johann-Jacob, *Garten-Beslustigungen*, c. 1783 *81, 335, 389*

Schynvoet, Simon, *Voorbeelden de Lusthof Cieraaden*, c. 1704 *227*

Smith, George, *Collection of Designs for Household Furniture*, 1808 *204*

Soane, Sir John, *Designs in Architecture, Consisting Of Plans, Elevations... For Temples... and other Buildings; for decorating Pleasure Grounds...*, 1797 *76/77, 96, 97*

Tod, George, *Plans, Elevations, & Sections of Hothouses, Green-Houses, an Aquarium, Conservatories etc. recently built*, 1812 *346, 347, 352, 353*

Van Der Groen, Johann, *The Netherlandish Gardener*, 1699 *12, 21, 26, 27, 306, 382/3*

Van Der Passe, Crispian, *Hortus Floridus, in quo rariorum & minus vulgarium florum Icones*, Eng/Fr trans., 1614 *22/23, 358, 359*

Van Laar, G., *Magazijn van Tuin-Sieraden*, 1802 ('Magazine of Garden Gems: a collection of Models taken partly from the major foreign publications') *74, 75, 82, 82, 123, 125, 140/1, 163, 193, 198, 208, 252, 257, 392*

Versailles, *Plans, Profils... de Versailles avec les bosquets et fontaines tels qu'ils sont à Présent*, Paris, (by D. Girard, P. Le Pautre et al.), 1715 *28/29, 292, 300, 316, 317, 320*

Versailles & Marly *(untitled volume)*, Paris, 1672–c. 1689 (after drawings by J. & P. Le Pautre, 1672/3 *220, 228/9, 234, 235, 236, 237, 293, 294, 295*

Visscher, Nicolaus, *(fl. late 17th century), Princely Palaces and Gardens of the Netherlands 42, 63, 124/5*

Wallis, N. *The Carpenter's Treasure: a Collection of Designs... for Temples*, 1793–95 *121*

Wrighte, William, *Grotesque Architecture, or Rural Amusement...*, 1768 (with several subsequent eds.) *85, 198, 209, 348*

Zocchi, Giuseppe *Vedute delle Ville, e d'Altri Luoghi della Toscana*, 1744 and 1757 *38, 39*

GLOSSARY

Allée
An avenue cutting through *bocage*, or clipped hedges, made as a ride or walk.

Arbour
A garden shelter open on one side, usually trained with climbers or creepers.

Arcade/ambulatio
A covered walkway, with one or both sides open via arches; as in the medieval cloister.

Balustrade
A stone fence of rails (usually of bulging form) and coping.

Belvedere
A raised platform or summer-house built as a lookout point.

Berceau
A covered walkway made of trelliswork, a usual feature of mid 16th-century/mid 18th-century French and Dutch gardens.

Bosquet
A densely planted block of trees, usually trimmed at the edges; through these clumps *allées* were driven, forming the architecture of the outer reaches of 17th-/18th-century parks; grouped bosquets (or *boscos* in Italian) were known as 'the Wilderness'.

Canal
Term used for any rectangular piece of water, sometimes a long canal-like stretch; a principal feature of early 18th-century gardens, often on the central axis.

Caryatid/telamon
Statuary in the form of supports, mainly for roofs of open-sided structures; the caryatid is in the female and the telamon in the male form.

Cascade
Waterfall in the form of a series of stepped falls, originating in 16th-century Italian gardens; more loosely used for a type of constructed waterfall as opposed to a natural one.

Chinoiserie
The 18th-century fashion for Chinese-style decoration, especially painted fretwork and bridges closely associated with Rococo; in France also called 'Anglo-Chinois'.

Clairvoyé
A 'see-through' in a screen wall or hedge; could be railings, or a cut-out, such as a circle.

Espalier/Cordon
A horizontal frame on which trees can be grown; espaliered fruit trees have their laterals trained in this form to fruit off alternate spurs; cordons have laterals removed and are trained to fruit off spurs from the leader only.

Exhedra
A covered area open on one side, usually semi-circular; in garden architecture, used as a feature for, for example, the seat at a conjunction of avenues.

Gazebo
May come from 'gaze-about': a look-out turret on a building, and from that, an open summerhouse, especially one with a second-storey viewing platform.

Grotto
Originally a cave; came to mean any natural or man-made underground room, with rock and shell decoration.

Herm
Antique busts or heads on squared pillars; after Hermes, messenger of the Gods. In Classical times, used to line roads, and so in gardens, to line avenues.

Icehouse
Construction, usually conical, of heavy brick- or stonework and often semi-underground, more for making ice for use in hot weather than for storing food.

Island bedding
Random flowerbeds set in the grass; a break with formal borders invented in Regency England (early 1800s).

Knot garden
A geometric bed of plants, including dwarf evergreen herbs and shrubs, in overlapping and interweaving strands, often edged with clipped box; popular in the Tudor period.

Loggia
An arcade open on one or both sides providing a shaded walkway; spread from Italy.

Pagoda
A multi-level gazebo or temple in the Chinese taste; following the Pagoda at Canton.

Parterre (de broderie)
A patterned garden of plants or turf made on a flat surface or terrace.

Patte d'oie
Literally 'goose's foot'; a web-shaped feature, where three or five avenues radiate from a central point.

Pergola
There are various definitions; here used to denote a cross-beam and pillar support for climbing plants, either as free-standing arches or in the form of a shelter.

Perron
The double staircase of the garden front of a house by which the principal rooms are reached.

Pleaching
A form of pruning much used in the 17th century and early 18th, by which the foliage of evenly spaced trees is densely woven and heavily pruned into geometric shapes, either from the ground or in their canopies, the trunks having been trimmed and trained to stilts. Hornbeam, beech, lime and sometimes chestnut were commonly used.

Rocaille
Rock and shell decoration attached to the walls of grottoes and niches, especially popular in the mid 18th-century Rococo period.

Rustic work
The fashion for weaving untrimmed branches and twigs into garden furniture.

Rustication
Rusticated stonework has chiselled or grooved blocks used in conjunction with a roughened surface, and was much employed for the ground floors of Renaissance Italian houses; it then became very popular for garden buildings, especially temples.

Temple
A small garden building or summer-house, often of classical form and with connotations of the antique.

Topiary
The art of pruning evergreens into geometrical, animal, or other shapes.

Treillage
Constructions of trelliswork, made of wooden laths, providing a frame for trees and climbers, or used as screens and walls; in early 18th-century gardens, especially, made into elaborate architectural constructions.

Wilderness
Outer reaches of large gardens or parks, thickly planted with trees; before the mid 18th-century in the form of clumps of *bocage* penetrated by long straight avenues with narrower serpentine walks between; later, the term denoted less formal plantings of woodland.

ACKNOWLEDGMENTS

The authors and publisher would like to extend special thanks to Bernard Shapero Rare Books, London, for making available many of the works from which the illustrations in this book have been taken. They would also like to thank the following for their help in making material available: Marlborough Rare Books, London, and Martin Trowbridge of the Trowbridge Gallery, London.

All the photographs for the illustration of the book were supplied by Philip de Bay from the Stapleton Collection, London, apart from the designs for tents on p. 201 which were kindly lent by the manufacturers, the Raj Tent Club, London.

The painstaking research of material and behind-the-scenes work by Sara Waterson are deserving of very special thanks; without her captions, bibliography and glossary the book would have been much less complete.